And Then She Said...

Sue
— every blessing
G Bell.

For CR & JE
lovers of stories,
lovers of God.

And Then She Said
True stories without morals

John L Bell

wild goose publications www.ionabooks.com

Copyright © 2024 John L Bell
All royalties from the sale of this book go to the
Wild Goose Resource Group of the Iona Community.

First published 2024 by
Wild Goose Publications
Suite 9, Fairfield
1048 Govan Road, Glasgow G51 4XS, Scotland
A division of Iona Community Trading CIC
Limited Company Reg. No. SC156678
www.ionabooks.com

ISBN 978-1-80432-357-1
Cover image © G_T_K.stock.adobe.com

The publishers gratefully acknowledge the support of the
Drummond Trust, 3 Pitt Terrace, Stirling FK8 2EY in producing this book.

All rights reserved. No part of this publication may be reproduced in any form or by any means, including photocopying, electronic publishing or any information storage or retrieval system, without written permission from the publisher via PLSclear.com.

John L. Bell has asserted his right in accordance with the Copyright, Designs and Patents Act, 1988, to be identified as the author of this work.

Overseas distribution
Australia: Willow Connection Pty Ltd, 1/13 Kell Mather Drive,
Lennox Head NSW 2478
New Zealand: Pleroma, Higginson Street, Otane 4170,
Central Hawkes Bay

Printed in the UK by Page Bros (Norwich) Ltd

Contents

Introduction 7

The Stories

1 The aerial 9
2 A foreign affair 12
3 Pornography 14
4 Naked 17
5 Dog lover 19
6 The girlfriend 21
7 Untimely guilt 24
8 Liberation 25
9 Driven 27
10 Hospitality 29
11 Colour supplements 31
12 The gifts 35
13 Pontifical salutation 37
14 Embargo 39
15 The apprentice angel 41
16 Eucharist 43
17 Mother's Day 45
18 A right royal occasion 47
19 Foreign tongues 49
20 Against the grain 51
21 Mothering 53
22 Forenames 55
23 The T shirt 57
24 The benefactor 60
25 Released from bondage 62

26 Telling it   64
27 The reel thing   66
28 Tears   68
29 Making it easy for others   70
30 Betty   72
31 The tug   74
32 Times! Citizen!   77
33 The mother of many   79
34 Good Friday   81
35 Isaiah   83
36 The gift   85
37 Baby care   87
38 Free at last   89
39 The Garden of Eden   91
40 No easy answer   93
41 The song   95
42 The sunbeam   97
43 The linguist   99
44 Jimmy   102
45 Mexico   104
46 Amnesty   107
47 The night visitor   110
48 Light in the tunnel   112
49 The bill   115
50 Transference   116

Introduction

This is not a 'holy' book written for religious people who like that kind of thing. The titles of the stories should be sufficient to dispel that notion. But it is, without apology, about life in its marvellous depth, absurdity and unexpectedness. And it is about faith, not as a crutch but as an adventure.

Unless you feel compelled to have some background, stop reading this page now! Leave it till later. Instead, choose a page randomly and sample the wares.

All these stories are true. And all these stories have been told several times in public. They only appear in print now because, over the past ten years or more, various people have asked whether I might ever publish such a collection.

They are not all about me, and they are not all about well-known people. The subjects who are alive and contactable have all given their assent, though some have asked for pseudonyms to be used. And as regards those whom I have been unable to contact directly because of either their death or no forwarding address, I have often given them an assumed name.

There are three reasons for this. Firstly, for me, these stories stand alone irrespective of the people involved. They represent that innate wisdom, humour, integrity and imagination which I believe God has given to all people. But in a celebrity culture, the experience of those who are not part of the popular narrative, nor desirous of entering it, often goes unrecognised.

Secondly, it fascinates me that many of the people who are associated with Jesus in the Gospels are unnamed – even the one who has the most verses devoted to her, the 'woman at the well'. But the absence of names does not detract from the value of the stories about the paralysed man, or the man born blind, or the Syro-Phoenician mother, or the child in whom Jesus saw the characteristics of God's kingdom.

But thirdly, and more cautiously, I have had the experience in the past where, having told one of these stories, a journalist begged to know how he might contact the person involved. I had no intention of starting a paper trail, so I never told him. The story is more important than the identity of either the subject or the author.

Many items in this collection involve women. Hence the title *And Then She Said*. In a world in which it is women who do most of the work and men who make most of the decisions, I feel bound, even in a small way, to try to rectify the imbalance. But that comes naturally, for when I look back on my life, I realise how many of the people who have nourished and enlarged my faith and religious affection have been female.

I am forever indebted to those who are featured in these pages. Their lives have touched mine and I am the better for it. But I also record my thanks to those whose requests encouraged the writing. And I am particularly grateful to Kathleen Grant, who not only suggested this project, but offered to give the manuscript a careful reading, sufficient for errors in punctuation, spelling, grammar and syntax to marvellously disappear. Any remaining imperfections are my responsibility.

I am also indebted, as ever, to Sandra Kramer and the staff of Wild Goose Publications for their encouragement and industry in editing and preparing my manuscript for its ultimate appearance in this book.

One
The aerial

416 Great Western Road was the address of a house which few people knew existed. The numeral appeared on one of the stone pillars on either side of a large metal fretwork gate. Behind it was a narrow corridor between two high windowless walls belonging to a four-storey tenement house on the right side and a church hall on the left.

Had you walked along the narrow lane, you would have come to a small courtyard on one side of which was a small house that abutted onto the ancillary rooms of the church.

The halls, ancillary accommodation and the caretaker's house were accretions added on after the congregation had established itself. It was one of the wealthy Glasgow West End churches which in the postwar era saw attendances gradually diminish as the wealthier locals moved from proximity to urban slums to the more exclusive suburbs. The demographic mix in the locality become ever more varied with many South Asians coming to live in the area along with university students from all over the United Kingdom and beyond.

By 1984 the church could no longer pay a part-time caretaker. When he and his family left, the house they occupied was available for rent. It had a tiny kitchen, and a damp living room and bathroom on the ground floor. At the top of a winding staircase was a tiny toilet which required users either to stoop or bang their head on the sloping ceiling, two small bedrooms and one much larger room.

This was the base for a volunteer scheme which my colleague Graham and I ran. It was the 'mother house' to which new full-time volunteers came for a month or more before being farmed out to other such houses in different parts of Glasgow and beyond.

They lived communally in groups of two or three with no title, and were required to exist on state benefit like the many unemployed people around them. The young male and female volunteers were encouraged to become familiar with their neighbourhoods, make themselves available to help with church or school groups, and try to discern what vocation and discipleship meant.

At one particular time, six of us lived together in the cramped accommodation. Graham and I shared one small bedroom and used the other as an office. The large upstairs room accommodated four very different teenagers, including a Protestant from Belfast and a Roman Catholic from Londonderry.

Despite the wholly inadequate accommodation, it was a great place to be. We learned what to do when another resident, who was a severe epileptic, had a seizure. Amazingly, he felt so relaxed in the environment that he – who would have two or three fits per day at home – might go for a month without incident. We learned what living in a constant state of danger and uncertainty felt like from the two boys who represented both sides of the religious divide in Northern Ireland. We ate together, entertained guests, and shared responsibility for a lovely mongrel dog called Pele. When asked about its pedigree, one standard answer was, 'It's a bit like Jesus. We've seen the mother but not the father.'

The house had nothing of value in it. We were all on the dole. Most of the furniture and much of our clothing was second hand. Despite that, we were burgled a couple of times; all that taken was a small and elderly portable television. Once gone it was never replaced.

Six months or so after its disappearance, along the narrow path at number 416 came an officer from the Television Licensing Authority. He knocked loudly at the door until Kieran, the only inhabitant at home that day, appeared and asked if he could help the man.

'Yes,' said the officer, 'I'm sure you can. You see, I have in my register information that this household has a television, but has not renewed the annual licence. So I've come to ask you to pay up.'

'No,' said Kieran, 'you have the wrong house. We don't have a television.'

'Well,' said the man, 'I have it on good authority that you do.'

'And I know from the experience of living here that we don't,' replied Kieran.

'Will you step out here a moment?' requested the official. So Kieran came out into the courtyard.

'If you look up there at the chimney stack,' the man said, pointing to the roof, 'you'll see an aerial with a long cable coming from it, right down the wall and through a small aperture into your downstairs room. You do have a television in there.'

'Sure,' replied Kieran, 'if you look through the window, you'll see that there's milk on the table. But that doesn't mean we have a cow in the kitchen.'

Two
A foreign affair

One Sunday after a service I had conducted in the English Reformed Church in Amsterdam, a man in his fifties hung around until most people had left. He then came up to me and gripped my hand tightly; he looked as if he had somehow been deeply moved.

I began to converse with him by suggesting that he was not a frequent attender. This was indeed the case. He explained how he came from Arizona in the USA, and had never been out of his country until this visit to Europe. He was in business, engaged in developing overseas markets for a successful engineering company in his home state. He had been abroad for almost a month, visiting interested parties in many of the capitals and larger cities in central and western Europe.

We chatted amicably and then he said, 'Pastor, the reason why I wanted to shake your hand is simply that I have longed for this day. Every Sunday I have gone to different English-speaking churches in the cities I've been visiting. I am a Bible-believing Christian, but I have always been disappointed until today: hours before I board a flight back to the States, I have heard the fundamentalist sermon for which I have been longing.'

I was taken aback, to say the least. I had never had that kind of compliment before, most certainly because, though I would call myself a biblical Christian, I do not subscribe to the kind of literalism of which my interlocutor was clearly an aficionado.

Puzzled, I tried to think of what could have been so significant in my preaching. And then it dawned on me. It might just have been the text I had chosen to expound. It was Luke 17:32 where Jesus says,

'Remember Lot's wife.'

Earlier in the service we had read, in Genesis 14, the story of how Lot had been commanded by angels to flee from the city of Sodom which God was keen to destroy. He and his family were told never to look back as they fled; but his wife did, and she 'turned into a pillar of salt'.

It's a story which many preachers avoid, but it's one that I love. And I have the notion that it was not my exposition of the story which so affected the man as the fact that here was a preacher who had taken an avoided biblical text seriously.

We bade each other goodbye. But two minutes later he was back with a copy of the *New English Bible* (which the church sold) in one hand and a pen in the other, begging me to write something which would commemorate his visit. I was unprepared for this, so simply inscribed on the first inside page the date, the words 'Remember Lot's wife', and my signature.

After he had gone I began to ponder whether his wife would be as knowledgeable about the Bible as he was; otherwise she might take 'Remember Lot's wife' not as a word from Jesus, but as evidence of a foreign affair.

Three
Pornography

For over thirty years I have collected postcards. Not scenes of seaside beaches, rural glades, urban streets or historic buildings, all in full colour. Rather, black and white postcards solely depicting people. Children of all ages laughing or crying, with mud on their clothes, mischief in their eyes, behaving well, behaving badly. Women in various states of dress and undress, drinking tea with each other, gazing down microscopes, working on building sites, slightly inebriate at parties. Men at work and leisure, digging up roads, drawing on a blackboard, developing their muscles in a gym, playing with their offspring.

I began collecting them to enliven Bible studies. I had become fed up with placid, anaemic depictions of a spineless Jesus and his associates as witnessed in Victorian stained-glass windows, children's storybooks and illustrations in the blessed King James Bible. My colleagues and I often worked with lay people who were hesitant to make any comment on scripture. But we discovered that if you asked them to select from a huge range of black and white photographs the one which seemed to them to best represent Zaccheus or Mary or the Woman at the Well or whoever, profound conversation often ensued.

Similarly, when taking preaching classes in seminaries, it was possible to challenge assumptions as to the age, status, character-type, affectations and even the weight of people whom Jesus met by using contemporary images to replace safe and dated representations. This nearly always caused upset to those who preferred to get their understanding of paralysed men or haemorrhaging women from reading books rather than relating to real people.

I took around fifty of these cards with me in 2019 when I was invited to work in Australia and New Zealand. It was both a very enjoyable and exhausting month abroad. I worked in a wide variety of contexts, constantly meeting unfamiliar people, and often travelling long distances between engagements.

On Thursday 30th of June, I made my way to my final destination, the small town of Springwood, in the Blue Mountains, some 72 kilometres west of Sydney. I put my case in the luggage rack of the busy commuter train, enjoyed the view while there was daylight, and thereafter snoozed on and off.

I was looking forward to being with people in the Uniting Church in Springwood. The engagement was not arduous: some workshops on global song, a memorial lecture remembering Noelene Martin, a great activist in the Fair Trade movement, and a sermon at the Sunday morning service.

When the train arrived at my destination, I discovered to my horror that my case had been stolen. It was not the best news with which to greet Graham and Leigh Gardiner, my hosts. There was, however, an attendant at the station to whom I gave information about the large suitcase which held everything apart from my travel documents, money and lecture notes. I told him when I last noticed the case, and how there had been some kerfuffle in the compartment a few stations back, but I had no idea what that was about. He noted everything, took Graham's mobile phone number, and said he'd pass on the information to the police.

My hosts were very kind. Once home, they gave me a large glass of whisky and provided surrogate essentials for ablutions. The next day, still in my travelling clothes, I led three short workshops on songs from different continents and walked around a Fair Trade exhibition. On the Saturday, still in the same garments, I led a fourth workshop and then, not wanting to deliver a sermon in an odoriferous condition, asked Graham if he could drive me to a clothing store so that I could supplement my diminished wardrobe.

I was on the point of withdrawing money from a cash machine in the shopping centre when Graham's mobile phone rang. The caller informed him that the case had been retrieved and was available for collection at the police station. Much relieved we drove there, and on entering the building I could clearly see my large grey case on the floor of a side room. I identified myself to the desk sergeant and signed the necessary recovery documents.

He then asked if we could go into the side room, but was insistent that Graham stayed outside. Once in the room, the sergeant shut the door firmly, and asked if I wanted to check through my case to ensure that nothing was missing. I declined on the basis that there was nothing of value, and that apart from being a bit bashed, everything looked intact.

He then asked me to sit down and in a more confidential tone said, 'Now, Mr Bell, this might be an awkward question. But would you by any chance have in your case a photograph of a family with no clothes on?'

'I do,' I replied. 'It's one of around fifty black and white postcards. It depicts a naked father lying face down on the ground. His wife is lying on top of him, then their four children atop their parents, arranged according to size. Oh, and there are no genitals showing.'

'Can I ask why this picture is in your possession?' asked the sergeant.

'I use it for Bible study,' I replied.

He was slightly taken aback, until I informed him of the ways in which the cards were used. I then asked him, 'Why did you pick out that specific card?'

He replied, 'We caught the thief with the help of CCTV footage. We knew him of old. When we entered his house he said, "OK. I admit I stole the case. But the porn doesn't belong to me."'

Four
Naked

There can be few talks which begin with the sentence, 'You have probably all seen me before, but the last time would be when I had no clothes on.'

Yet these, or words to that effect, were spoken at a conference of Presbyterian Women which I attended in Toronto in 2014. Hardly had the statement been made when on a screen appeared one of the most iconic photographs of the 20th century. It won the World Press Photo of the Year in 1972 and in no small way assured the life of the nine-year-old Vietnamese girl whose image was central.

She is Phan Thi Kim Phuc, and in the photograph she is totally naked, clearly distressed and fleeing from napalm which an American bomber had dropped on her village of Trang Bang in South Vietnam. Kim Phuc suffered third-degree burns, and was almost given up for dead, but eventually received life-saving treatment.

She told the story of her disfigurement, of her gradual healing, of her life of reintegrating herself into society, and spoke with great clarity and affection for her ardent listeners. We heard how, during a period of despair, she found a copy of a New Testament in a library, and became a Christian through reading it.

Her study abroad in Cuba, her marriage, her daring dash to seek political asylum in Canada, and her subsequent work and family life are all recorded in her biography, *The Girl in the Picture*.

In her talk in Toronto, she indicated how her conversion to Christianity did not automatically guarantee a trouble-free faith. What she found almost offensive was the command of Jesus not just to love your neighbour as yourself, but to 'love your enemy; bless those who persecute you'. She resisted this, understandably, given how her life had almost ended when American war machinery dispensed flammable liquid over her village.

Then the day came when she was invited to speak at the Vietnam Memorial in Washington DC. This meant surrendering the hate in her heart against those who had slaughtered her innocent fellow Vietnamese citizens. But she accepted the engagement, spoke with deep conviction about the need for peace and reconciliation, and expressed her forgiveness for a man who had been in the American Air Force and engaged in bombing her country.

Five
Dog lover

In October 1968, Lord George MacLeod, the founder of the Iona Community, was elected Rector of Glasgow University. This honorary post is found only in the four ancient Scottish universities. It is reckoned to originate from the practice in mediaeval Bologna whereby a sector of the student body had the right to vote for the titular head of the University.

Up to the present day, every three years there is an election among students in St Andrews, Glasgow, Aberdeen and Edinburgh to vote for their preferred candidate from a range of promoted personalities, usually from the world of politics or academia.

Prior to his installation, George took part in a debate in the Students' Union in which a number of students and social luminaries also spoke. The subject for discussion was the role of religion in contemporary society. In the course of the evening a seasoned student debater spoke in these terms:

'Lord MacLeod, I want to say first of all that I am very interested in heaven. I'm also very fond of my wee dog Freddie. I know that he'll probably die before me, but I'm seriously worried about whether or not we'll meet again on the other side of time. So I'd like to ask you whether or not there will be dogs in heaven.'

At this, George drew himself up to his full height and responded in stentorian fashion:

'Young man, you'll be lucky if you get into heaven in your shirt tails never mind with your damned little Pomeranian!'

Later, during his installation address, he offered a critique of the different faculties within the university, commenting on each with a mixture of perceptiveness and wit. When it came to the Faculty of Medicine, he told this story:

There was a young man from the Highlands who had been so

impressed by the skill and kindness of his family doctor that he decided to pursue a career in medicine.

On returning to his home village for the Christmas holidays, after his first term as a student, he paid a visit to his GP who was keen to know of his protégé's progress. During their conversation, the veteran doctor asked the young man whether he was still keen on going into general practice.

'No,' replied the boy, 'I've decided that I'd like to specialise in the nose.'

'You mean Ear, Nose and Throat?' asked the doctor.

'No,' replied the boy, 'just the nose.'

'And tell me, young man,' replied the GP, 'exactly to which nostril do you intend to devote your professional career?'

Six
The girlfriend

Gaby de Wil was a well-loved and devout believer who worshipped in the Roman Catholic church of the Beguinage in Central Brussels. The area in which the church is set is one of several cloisters similarly named in the Francophone parts of Belgium, and known as Begijnhofs in the Flemish-speaking regions of Belgium and in the Netherlands. The Beguines were a lay community of women who lived in cloister houses and were committed to works of charity.

One Saturday afternoon at the Vigil Mass, a rather unkempt boy appeared in the building and sat among the forty or more people who regularly attended this Eucharist. Someone must have welcomed him, sufficient for him to return, looking even more unkempt, the next Sunday.

Gaby had no hesitation in speaking to the boy after the liturgy. She learned that he was called Jean-Pierre, and that he was homeless after being thrown out of the house by his parents. She encouraged him to come back the following Sunday; and meanwhile, with the help of a friend in the congregation, managed to secure accommodation for the young man.

In due course, their acquaintanceship grew into friendship. Gaby invited him for meals and gradually learned more about his life. His parents had rejected him because he had told them he was gay. Made homeless and having no means to support himself, he had become a rent boy, offering sexual services to older men in return for money.

Before long, when another person in the congregation identified a job vacancy which suited Jean-Pierre, he started regular employment and gradually became a fondly-valued member of the Beguinage congregation. He did not restrict himself to the Vigil

Mass, but often attended the main Sunday morning Eucharist as well. In time, and out of conviction, he enquired as to whether he, baptised as a child, might be confirmed into full membership of the Christian Church. This happened within a year at the Eve of Easter.

As he became more confident in himself, and more trusting with Gaby, he confided one day that he had gone to a sexual health clinic for a check-up. It resulted in him being advised that he was HIV positive. He had AIDS, and this was before antiretroviral drugs were available to people similarly infected.

Inevitably, as time passed, he became weaker. He had to forfeit his job, but kept his friendship with the people of the Beguinage, until the progress of the illness required him to have full-time care in a hospice.

Once or twice a week, Gaby would take two tram journeys across Brussels in order to visit him. She brought things he might like to eat. But more importantly she talked to him, sang to him, prayed with him, told outrageous stories to make him laugh, and always affirmed her affection for him.

In due course he died. After Mass in the church, he was buried in a local graveyard. Many people from the congregation attended both services to honour his life, thank God for his presence, and pray for his soul.

At the end of the burial service, as people went on their way, Gaby noticed a woman who was lingering by the graveside. She approached her, and gently enquired as to whether she might be Jean-Pierre's mother. 'I am,' replied the woman with audible grief in her voice.

After identifying herself and sharing some conversation, Gaby said, 'Madame, I wish you to know two things for your consolation. Your son Jean-Pierre died peacefully, and he died as a Christian. That is why we were all here.'

Jean-Pierre died aged 22; Gaby de Wil was almost four times his age. But she had been for him a surrogate grandmother, a confidante, a constant encourager and, despite her age, his only girlfriend.

Seven
Untimely guilt

I had met Maurice twenty minutes previously, when he and his parents and siblings arrived at the church for his grandmother's funeral. I had already spoken to his father but not to any other family members. The door of the church, just before the start of the funeral, was not the best venue for a substantial conversation. But I managed to find out from his father a little about each of the children, and learned that Maurice, aged seventeen, was hoping to be a journalist.

They took their places in the church. The building began to fill up with the motley assortment of believers and doubters you get at any funeral. The organ had begun playing and I began to robe.

I looked over my notes and checked that I had the name of the deceased as she was both properly and commonly known. I underlined a note in my text to make sure that I told the congregation where the cremation would take place and, after it, the reception.

I was about to leave the vestry when the door burst open and in came Maurice, weeping copiously. I was a little thrown as it was starting time, not the best moment to begin grief counselling. But I asked the boy to sit down, put my hand on his shoulder and said something like,

'It's not very easy when people you love die, especially when it's someone close to you like your grandmother.'

'But it's not my grandmother,' wept Maurice. I began to wonder whether he was alluding to being genetically unrelated to the deceased. And then he burst out, 'It's not about my granny. It's my girlfriend. I've been cheating on her.'

Eight
Liberation

My mother had a difficult relationship with her own mother as long as that dear lady was alive. This resulted in a long-term sense of guilt once Mary, aged sixty-four, had gone to her rest.

She could never quite understand the cause of the awkwardness between them. Was it because she was 'a little late one' who diverted Mary's attention from her beloved son Jack, who was a decade older? Or was it that she, Marion, my mother, was a mischievous child and an awkward adolescent who married a man of whom Mary disapproved? Whatever the cause, she knew her mother's censure, criticism and disdain as a reality before Mary's death, and as an uncomfortable memory thereafter.

One day when she was in her late sixties, my mother had a phone call from a man who began by saying, 'Hello, May. I'm your cousin Jerry.'

She had not seen or heard of Jeremiah Johnston for over forty years. Yet here he was, his voice a little Anglicised through living most of his life in southern England, but still peppered with distinctive Ayrshire vowels. The means whereby he connected with her are of little interest, but for my mother the re-establishment of this familial friendship was of very significant value.

Being a widow and having a son in London, it was easy for her to arrange an initial visit with Jerry. She chose wisely to stay with my brother, rather than risk being a house guest with people she didn't know well. But the visit was a great success, and until she died, my mother frequently shared telephone calls and visits with Jerry and his wife.

In the course of their conversations, Jerry revealed that their common Aunt Babs, Mary's youngest sibling, was alive and fairly well, living in a care facility around ten miles from my mother's home. Marion had presumed that her aunt had gone to Barbados and never returned. Given the information of Babs' whereabouts, it was not long before she arranged to meet her.

Babs was in her late eighties, very frail but still mobile, and with a slow cancer which did not cause her much discomfort. For the last two years of Babs' life, the reconnected aunt and niece enjoyed regular conversation with each other, catching up on almost five decades of silence.

On one occasion, when she had the measure of her aunt, Marion said to her, 'Aunt Babs, what was my mother really like?' Babs drew her breath for a moment and then said, 'Well Marion, let me just say that when our Mary brought to our family home her new beau, John Lamberton, we who were her sisters said to each other, "What's a nice boy like John Lamberton doing with our Mary?"'

That, basically, was enough. It let Marion know that her mother had always been an awkward customer. It did not just assuage her feeling of guilt, it eradicated it.

Nine
Driven

The voice at the other end of the phone was female, but the name was not one I recognised. She said she had heard that we were trying to encourage music-making in churches in Scotland. I agreed that was one of our pursuits.

She then went on to say that she was coming to Scotland in a car which she wanted to get rid of, as there was a new one soon coming her way. And she wanted to give her old car to us to help with our work.

It all seemed too good to be true, and I remember doubting whether this was an authentic offer, as we had a number of friends, male and female, who were convincing mimics. But I said that if that was what she wanted to do, we would be very happy to accept her gift. Accordingly I gave our address and she suggested that she might come to our house the following Thursday morning around eleven o' clock.

Neither Graham, my colleague, nor I thought any more of it. I don't think we even spoke of it again. It was such an unlikely thing; indeed it would be a bit of a joke, especially if the woman knew anything about us.

But on the stated day, and at the stated time, she arrived. She was a slender blonde-haired young woman with the most charming manner, coming from a presumably more comfortable residence in London than our rather battered rented caretaker's cottage next to a highly polluted arterial road in Glasgow. We invited her in, made some coffee and conversed for a while, and then she handed over the keys and some documents relating to a well-preserved Honda Accord.

The awkward thing was that neither Graham nor I could drive. Nor did either of us have the faintest desire to take lessons. But there were other people we worked with who did drive, and the car became a very helpful asset in the early stages of our work.

And the young woman? She was completely unknown to us. Bernadette Farrell, one of the most widely-respected Roman Catholic liturgical composers, was not a household name at that time in Protestant Scotland. But now those who sing concur that her setting of Psalm 139, *O God you search me and you know me,* is one of the most beautifully crafted and meaningful texts that Christians of all persuasions in Britain are glad to sing.

Ten
Hospitality

Coby Burger never married, but led a life of great contentment. She was brought up in an Evangelical Christian tradition in the Netherlands, and for most of her working life she cleaned an insurance office in central Amsterdam.

In 1942 her life was to change significantly because of a knock on her door. When she opened it, there stood before her a very frightened-looking Jewish woman in her mid-thirties, about the same age as Coby. She asked whether Coby might be able to help her.

'My husband is in Austria, my daughter is in France and they are taking away my people.'

This was an allusion to the pogrom happening all over Europe in countries occupied by German forces. Amsterdam had a large Jewish population and the city was the involuntary host to a considerable contingent of the German army.

Coby had never been confronted with such a request for help. But she invited the woman into her home, made tea for her and engaged in conversation. After a while she said,

'You can stay here with me. You should say that you are a cousin of mine from the north of the country and you have come here looking for work. But I will need to find you different clothes. You are dressed like a Jewish lady. You'll need to change your appearance. And, though I will not require this of you, it might help if you come to the church I attend. That way there will be less suspicion.'

Until the end of the war, the Jewish woman lived with Coby. And when the war was over, she discovered that both her husband and her daughter had been killed by the Nazis.

Although I had got to know Coby Burger during the two years

in which I lived in Amsterdam, I was unaware of this magnificent act of kindness. And I would never have known about it had I not been in the city one summer in the 1990s doing holiday cover for the minister of the English Reformed Church. While I was there, Coby's niece phoned to say that her aunt had died, and to ask if I would take her funeral.

In the conversations which we shared, I became aware that Coby had been much more that a timid-looking elderly woman who spoke English reasonably well and occasionally went for holidays to Norfolk.

I realised that she was probably the bravest woman I had ever met. For had the occupying forces learned that she was providing a safe refuge for a Jewish woman, she might well have been on the train to Auschwitz or Belsen along with her guest.

Coby had taken seriously the words of Jesus that you have not only to love your neighbour as yourself, but also to love the one whom others would regard as your enemy.

Eleven
Colour supplements

My late colleague Graham Maule was a hoarder, though he would have called himself a collector, or an enthusiast for *objets trouvés*.

One item of which he had amassed hundreds of specimens was the colour supplement which many Sunday newspapers published on glossy paper. These had more comment and personality items than hard news, and contained pages on gardening, cooking and self-help, as well as advertisements.

It was his habit when travelling any distance by train on a Sunday to walk through the compartments within minutes of arriving at his destination, and rescue from oblivion any visible colour supplements cast aside or left behind by passengers. These he would stuff into a bag and bring home to be added to already existing piles of this commodity.

As with the piles of junk which his then girlfriend and he had deposited in the courtyard of his dwelling place, the intention was that sometime they would be used in a 'project'. In retrospect it is clear that this intentional accumulation of stuff was a harbinger of his emerging identity as an 'installation artist'. It was on a very cold February night that one of these uses was exhibited in public.

A church in an affluent neighbourhood asked my colleagues and me whether we would be interested in spending an evening with members of the congregation exploring personal spirituality. After a long discussion Graham and I agreed on a plan which involved his great collection of magazines.

Along with some of our full-time volunteers we trudged through deep snow from the train station to the church hall bearing the acres of newsprint in bags and boxes. We must have looked an unlikely facilitation team, as years later someone admitted that just prior to our arrival, someone burst into the hall to announce that 'a crowd of hippies are coming up the path'.

Once we had arrived and were introduced, Graham outlined that the audience of around fifty people would be put into three groups. Each group would have a pile of colour supplements, a large A3 piece of white paper, and a supply of scissors and glue. Each group was to reflect on a different person of the Holy Trinity – God the Creator, Jesus and the Holy Spirit.

They had all individually to peruse the magazines and pick out pictures which for them spoke of God, Jesus or the Spirit, according to their group. Once individuals had made a selection, the group together was to choose between six and eight images which were deemed to be the most evocative. The only conditions were that crosses, doves and printed words could not be used. This was to avoid clichéd images or a flight into intellectualism.

This was not exactly the kind of spiritual exploration that these innocent people had been expecting. Nor was cutting scraps out of printed magazines the kind of activity to which the largely professional group of people were accustomed. But before long they were all engaged. In due course, Graham called for the groups to make their choice of favoured images, which were then to be stuck on the pieces of A3 paper, each one being headed either God the Creator, Jesus or Holy Spirit.

When we were all back together, I asked each group to explain why they had chosen certain images to appear in their collage, and began to explore whether they were helpful or unhelpful to faith.

The Holy Spirit collage was unforgettable. The cut-outs included a computer, a flame, an old woman and a puppy dog wrapped in Andrex toilet paper. (This last was an advertisement for the brand.)

Individuals gave good reasons for their choice of picture. The person who chose the flame alluded to Pentecost and the coming of the Spirit. Whoever chose the computer did so because it was a storehouse of knowledge, as was the Holy Spirit. Someone said that recently the church's minister had indicated that, in Hebrew, the Holy Spirit was a female noun, hence the choice of a wise old woman.

And then there was the puppy dog. I asked why it had been chosen, and a very respectable, well dressed gentleman said, 'Well we were told we couldn't have a dove, so we wanted another representation of the gentleness of the Spirit.'

With no aforethought, I continued,

'Tonight we are in a reasonably affluent environment. But not far from here is Smeaton Street, located in a poor area near where some of our volunteers live. It seems that in Smeaton Street there are two major irritants. The one is that windows are frequently broken, and though the inhabitants pay their rent, it seems to take a long while before the District Council gets them repaired. The other menace is an infestation of rats, such that mothers are reluctant to leave their babies in their prams, even for a short while, for fear they might get bitten.

'Now, if you were going to pray for the people in Smeaton Street tonight and you had in your mind a gentle image of the Spirit, symbolised here by the puppy dog, what would you pray?'

There was a silence, and then an elderly lady said,

'I would pray that God sent the Holy Spirit to calm the anxieties in the minds of those who lived there until the time came when their present difficulties were ameliorated.'

I thanked her and then asked,

'Now what would you pray if your image of the Spirit was fire?'

And the man who previously explained that choice suddenly said with some passion:

'If the Holy Spirit was like fire, I would have to pray that the Spirit infuriated the local inhabitants such that they went together to the City Hall, demanded to see their councillors, and did not leave until they had a guarantee that within a week all the windows would be repaired and the rats would be eradicated.'

And then he sat back looking rather surprised that he had spoken these words.

I said to him, 'Do you really mean this?' He replied, 'Yes.'

And then he said, 'If the Holy Spirit is like fire, that is what I would need to pray.'

Twelve
The gifts

Chitra Karki from Nepal's capital city, Kathmandu, worked for several years as a volunteer in Scargill House and Lee Abbey conference centres. He developed fond friendships with people in different parts of Britain, and sent back to Nepal most of his pocket money, to the fledgling independent church to which he belonged.

Since his conversion to Christianity at his uncle's funeral, he had a strong desire to serve the church as an evangelist, but felt that his limited biblical knowledge was insufficient for this vocation. He discussed this with me when I visited Kathmandu, and I offered to try to find an establishment where he might study. I was flying soon after to Australia and there I was sure that a friend I had made, who was the president of a Baptist College, might be of assistance.

She did indeed offer a place; but Chitra said that, if possible, he would prefer to study in the United Kingdom. No mention of inclement weather put him off; he had grown up in the Himalayas and knew how to cope with both cold and heat. Eventually, through fundraising by people in England and Scotland, and with the generous cooperation of the Glasgow Bible College, he was able to fulfil his desire to study the scriptures.

During the first year Sharda, his wife, remained in Nepal, but both were keen that she should join him for the second year of his master's programme. They found accommodation in a multicultural area in the south side of the city and became friends with a Scottish couple who had a long connection with Nepal.

When his time at the Bible College was coming to a close, Chitra and Sharda were keen to show their appreciation to people who had befriended them and funded them. Their desire was to cook a traditional Nepalese meal, and they asked whether they could use the substantial flat in which I lived to host the occasion.

They arrived around ten o'clock in the morning and prepared and cooked assiduously until four thirty, finishing in time to greet their friends who began arriving shortly before five.

The smell alone was sumptuous, and everyone was thrilled at the range of traditional dishes they produced, a feast which put the offerings of the local Asian curry houses in the shade.

As they were leaving, Sharda gave me a small lightweight parcel in which I found a beautiful red artificial flower with a green stem and leaves. Chitra indicated that she had made it herself from rubbish found in the streets around the area where they lived in Glasgow. I was very touched by such a personal token of their kindness. But I also felt rather ashamed.

Three years previously, when I visited Kathmandu, I had been invited to dinner in their home. They had recently got married and were sharing a small house with Chitra's sister. I had decided to take a wedding present for them, and bought a fairly expensive, colourful and curiously-shaped glass bowl.

When I entered their home, it was clear that they lived in comparative poverty and that an expensive glass bowl was the last thing they needed to have in a house which had nothing by way of ornamentation. The shame I felt then came back with great force when Sharda gave me her hand-made flower. I had given them a useless artefact which spoke of extravagance. She had given me something which spoke of careful artistry, simplicity and beauty. It remains my favourite possession.

Thirteen
Pontifical salutation

In 1982, Pope John Paul II came to Glasgow along with his 'popemobile', the motorised vehicle which enabled him to circumnavigate the vast crowds who came to see him in Bellahouston Park, as they did all over the world during his papacy. It was a memorable – almost iconic – image of a person of world renown coming within touching distance of millions of people on a buggy.

Around the same time Robert Armstrong began to be compromised by the effect multiple sclerosis was having on his body. His young wife felt unable to cope with a husband who had a degenerative illness, and so ended the marriage not long after the diagnosis was made. Rob then lived alone, but – when he became unable to work – he was ably assisted by a range of carers, drivers and friends who kept him active and engaged.

He had long wanted to visit the island of Iona, but – like many Scots – had never done so. We discussed the possibility, and eventually he came to a week-long event in what was called the Youth Camp. It was accommodation adapted from four huts which the workers had occupied during the rebuilding of the Abbey, and which increasingly bore the marks of age and decay. It had bed space for forty-four people in metal-framed bunks which were located in four dormitories with one cold tap between ten or twelve people. The space between the huts was covered not with paving but pebbles.

This posed what seemed a formidable problem for Rob when he arrived, as he was unsteady on his feet and moved with the help of sticks. Paving was fine for him, but not the unevenness of stones. But when a wheelchair was found, people were keen to take turns to move him across the site and help him manage the two stairs from ground level into the huts.

Rob was a very endearing character. At the week he attended he was the oldest of the residents. Most were between sixteen and twenty-four. He was thirty at this time, but his geniality and winsomeness made him a favourite. Indeed four boys from Eton College, who had never met anyone who was so disabled, vied with each other to push his wheelchair up and down the path to the Abbey when he attended worship there.

On the last evening, there was a dance and concert in the village hall. This was not a very sophisticated event. The music for dancing – a mixture of Scottish folk music and rock – came from a record player; and the entertainment was provided solely by the variable efforts and abilities of people who were staying in the Youth Camp and Abbey centres. So there was a predictable pot-pourri of the talented and the trying in a mixed diet of songs, poems, sketches and general silliness.

A singer had just finished, and, as the clapping died down, people became aware of an unexpected diversion. A horn began to sound loudly,. Then came requests to clear a way, as into the hall and around its perimeter came Rob in a motorised buggy, decked in a make-do white cassock with a mitre on his head. He circumnavigated the audience doing nothing more than smiling and blessing everyone, and he disappeared as quickly as he had arrived. It was the most transforming gesture which only he could have carried out with such authenticity.

Fourteen
Embargo

In the history of both Canada and the USA, the significance of the church in educational provision cannot be underrated. The Roman Catholic Church in particular built institutions of primary and secondary education, teacher training colleges and even universities.

Many women who took the veil entered orders with a particular commitment to the education – mental, physical and spiritual – of the sons and daughters of Catholic parents. And many of the orders were able to extract vast amounts of money from wealthy Catholics who wanted to preserve their religious pedigree in education.

These orders, during the holiday breaks, would routinely hold conferences in the larger convents or mother-houses, bringing together teachers who represented different disciplines to update them on the syllabuses and help them develop classroom and teaching skills.

Religious education conferences, when advertised, always had a sizeable response, as it was a compulsory subject. Priests in the local church could not always be relied on to offer classroom instruction as well as chaplaincy work. In the post Vatican Two era, with the revision of the liturgy, the diversification of musical styles, and the higher profile of Catholic social teaching, it was important that the schools moved in the vanguard rather than rearguard of church practice.

Years ago I met a distinguished professor of religious education who, though not a Roman Catholic, was widely acclaimed by high school teachers in that tradition. He related his experience as a guest speaker at a conference of a religious order, held in a convent in Washington DC.

The professor, whom we will call Albert, was asked if he would like to stay in the convent guest house, which he did. He attended morning prayer each day, dined with the sisters, and lectured for one session every morning and afternoon. In the evenings, he was wont to frequent the convent lounge and avail himself of Catholic hospitality.

The good sisters were so enamoured by his geniality, his teaching, and his interest in their work, that several of them approached the mother superior. Knowing that the local bishop would be coming to celebrate Mass on the coming Friday, they asked whether the superior might intercede by asking the bishop to make a special dispensation and allow the professor to join with the sisters in receiving the sacrament during the Eucharist.

The superior was favourable to their request, and contacted the bishop, but to no avail.

On the Friday morning at 11 o'clock, the becloaked nuns entered and filled the convent chapel. The bishop, with a young priest assisting him, led the liturgy of the Mass, and preached what was generally regarded as a rather presumptuous sermon. He was not a religious education specialist, and would have been better sticking to the lectionary readings of the day, rather than offering untested advice as to how best to represent the Christian faith to believing and unbelieving students.

When it came to the Eucharist, the bishop consecrated the bread and wine, and served both himself and his assistant. They then came to the altar steps with paten and chalice in their respective hands, ready to offer the body and blood of the Saviour to his devoted servants.

And not one of them moved.

Fifteen
The apprentice angel

At a conference centre near Edinburgh, I was invited to do some sessions on enabling people to teach new songs. Among those in the group I met was an unlikely participant. She hadn't come for the course, but the warden of the centre suggested she might join those who had signed up.

As part of my then practice, I would – at the beginning of the proceedings – go round the group and say to them, one by one, '[Name], you have the voice of an apprentice angel.' This was said almost tongue in cheek when it came to Nell. She was a recovering alcoholic with a passion for cigarettes and a voice which was of variable pitch, but could cut glass. However, I said it, and she stayed the course and learnt a variety of songs which, as she came from a very Protestant part of Scotland, might have been of little interest to her. One of these was a *Kyrie* from Ukraine, which people learned in three-part harmony.

A month later, Nell telephoned me with a request to come to her church on a Friday evening to help people to pray. This church was in an area which, at that time, was the most impoverished public housing estate in Western Europe. The group that met on Friday evenings comprised a mixture of people, some of whom were recovering alcoholics or drug abusers, some former prison inmates, others folk living in poverty who were vulnerable in the community.

I went with some trepidation, taking nothing with me but a large white candle and a small Bible. As I entered the meeting room in the church, I immediately sensed that the people gathered were impoverished: sad and regretful histories were etched in the lines on their faces. I felt wholly inadequate. Perhaps sensing my apprehension, Nell spoke up. 'John,' she said, 'don't worry about the singing. They can all do that *Kyrie*. I told them I was an apprentice angel, and if I could do it, so could they.'

I began by mentioning that one of the lovely things Jesus said was that he was the Light of the World. Because of this I was going to light the candle and put it in the middle of the circle in which we were gathered. I asked that the ceiling lights be put out, and suggested that people look at the candle while I repeated the words that Jesus used about himself. Then we would sing the *Kyrie*, and when we stopped, anyone who had something they wanted to say to Jesus could say it looking at the candle. Then we would sing the *Kyrie* again and after every time someone spoke.

It was a sublime experience; it seemed that time stood still. And it seemed as if raw and nicotined voices were the heavenly choir. Such prayers were said, the honesty and earnestness of which I will never forget: a man praying that the following day his brother-in-law would not remove furniture from his house; a woman entreating God to let the judge know next week that she was a changed person, now capable of looking after her children. And many more.

And all this happening because of the faith and commitment of a woman whom I had been reticent to call an apprentice angel.

Sixteen
Eucharist

Holy Week on Iona is a great time. The ten-day retreat from Palm Sunday to Easter Monday changes each year according to the leadership team. But there is always a common pattern for the celebration of the Triduum – the period which covers Maundy Thursday to Easter Day.

The Maundy Thursday communion frequently takes place not in the Abbey Church, but in the Refectory – the upper room. The story of the betrayal of Jesus may then be read in the darkness of the cloisters. Then the congregation gathers in the nave, looking at the ancient building ablaze with light, until candle after candle is doused during the reading of Psalm 22, and the light turns to darkness.

On Good Friday there is usually a celebration of the Stations of the Cross, beginning on the seashore, and gradually moving towards the Abbey where the crude processional cross is set up before the altar. People are invited to come to terms with what in their life needs to be amended, forgiven or surrendered in the face of Christ's willingness, through his death, to redeem all things. Thereafter a liturgical action may enable people to symbolically express their penitence.

Friday evening often sees worshippers gather in small groups in unusual places – in store cupboards, in hidden corners of outbuildings – this in imitation of the disciples who scattered after the crucifixion. In such hideouts a common short liturgy is shared.

On the Saturday evening, the vigil service moves at midnight from darkness into light, as the story of the women going to the tomb reaches its climax, and the bell rings and candles are rekindled. There may be joyful dancing and – on occasion – an aurora borealis has been seen in the northern sky, as nature celebrates the risen Christ.

Then, on Easter Day, there is the Sunday Eucharist with a packed Abbey bringing together staff, guests, local residents and day visitors – the believers and the curious, the long in the tooth and the new to faith.

One year after this worship service, I met a woman outside the bookshop. She was somewhere in her late fifties, and had a look of contentment about her. I asked her if she regularly came to Iona, and she said, 'Only at Easter.' I asked her if there was a particular reason for this and then she said:

'I am the mother of four children. One of my sons, now aged twenty-five, is gay. He always has been and always will be. I am a cradle Catholic and I know the teaching of my church regarding homosexuality. I don't agree with it, and here's why.

'Since his mid-teens, Gerald seemed to turn in on himself. Other boys he ran about with were beginning to go out with girls. He was envious of them, and envious of the girls because he would have loved to spend Saturday evenings with the boys in his class, just mucking around.

'After school, when he began to work, he would get teased because he didn't have a girlfriend. I knew what the trouble was; he knew I knew, but neither of us could do anything about it. And then three years ago he met Ryan, and my son has never been happier; his sister and brothers are all happy for him, and so am I. And I love Ryan, because he has brought companionship and affection into Gerald's life in a way no one else could.

'In the church I go to, we have a priest who is over-fond of accusing gay people of being "inherently disordered". My son and his partner could never be described in this degrading way. If anyone is inherently disordered, it's that priest. So on Easter morning I have no desire to receive holy communion from the hands of a man who makes such an accusation. That is why I come here.'

Seventeen
Mother's Day

In the United Kingdom, the celebration commonly called 'Mother's Day' is more appropriately referred to as Mothering Sunday. Its origin is in the mediaeval practice of having one Sunday in the year when people would return to the church in which they were baptised and/or reared.

In the United Kingdom, it is a moveable feast determined by the date on which the fourth Sunday in Lent falls. In other countries which hold the event on a Sunday, its celebration is more predictable.

One particular year, I was working in Gibraltar, and on the Sunday morning decided to go to the nearest church to my hotel. It happened to be the Anglican Cathedral. Midway through the service, a venerable and rather dusty senior priest ascended the pulpit stairs, and in a plummy voice which betrayed his privileged upbringing, he began,

'My dear people, today is Mother's Day. So today I am going to speak to the mothers, because they deserve it. But if you are not a mother, you can either listen along or snooze for the duration of my homily.'

I felt in no small way discomfited. I looked around. There were no children, no women under the age of 50, a spattering of elderly couples and a number of adults, male and female, sitting on their own. It seemed as if the majority of us had been given a dispensation to slumber in church. This was welcome since the homily was patronising and dire.

Two months later I was working in Sydney, Australia. On the Sunday, which happened to be the second Sunday in May, I had no engagements. So I decided that I would attend morning worship at the first church I came to when I left my lodgings. It happened to be a Roman Catholic one where Mass was about to begin at 11.00am.

It was a bright modern building, with a good-sized congregation. As I looked at the bulletin handed to me at the door, I saw it was headed

> Sunday May 12th. Mother's Day.

The spirit groaned within me. I thought that if Gibraltar was bad, this was bound to be worse. But I was determined I should thole what I might not enjoy.

During the entrance hymn, the priest, a man in his early fifties, processed to the altar. At the conclusion of the hymn, he greeted the congregation with these words:

'A very warm welcome to you all, especially to whoever may be visiting among us.

'You will notice from the bulletin that this is Mother's Day. If you have come here expecting I will be extolling women who have borne children, you have come to the wrong place.

'Today we are not here to celebrate mothers. We are here to thank God that we have all been mothered … some by our birth mothers, some by adopted mothers, some by our grandmothers, some by our fathers or carers; and pray God we have all been mothered by the church.'

For a moment I pondered whether I should shout, 'Hallelujah', or run to the altar and kiss the priest for being so inclusive.

Eighteen
A right royal occasion

What became the Wild Goose Resource Group began with four of us – Chris, Christine, Graham and I – on the dole. There wasn't much money for developments in church music or liturgy. But because we believed it was important to work in this field, we survived for the first two years on Social Security and then on a very low salary.

In our second year, a request came (probably from the then British Council of Churches) for one of us to represent the Iona Community in a planning meeting for a national church service to celebrate the forthcoming Year of Peace. We agreed that Christine should go.

She arrived in Church House, Westminster, and was shown into a committee room where all those gathered, apart from herself, were men. Several were wearing dull clerical attire, which made her – who favours bright colours – look positively flamboyant.

The meeting was convened by an Anglican clergyman who, after opening prayers, suggested that those around the table should introduce themselves to each other. And so they did, citing impeccable credentials of this variety:

'I'm the archdeacon of ABC and have been involved in several state occasions of this kind.'

'I'm a senior lecturer in liturgy at the 123 college, which I came to after my postgraduate studies at Yale.'

'I'm the Dean of XYZ. We just had a visit from HRH two months ago. Splendid occasion, and a charming lady if I may say so.'

'I'm a PhD student presently studying ceremonial rituals in the pre-Reformation church.'

And last of all:

'I'm Christine Reid. I come from Glasgow and I'm unemployed.'

There was an embarrassed hush. But to recover momentum,

the convener began to outline how this was a very significant ecumenical and national occasion. It would take a great deal of planning and, being of such a high national profile, it would probably have to happen in somewhere like Westminster Abbey. Such a space would be needed to accommodate the array of people coming. There would inevitably be processions – of the clergy, the armed forces, parliament and the Crown.

At this point, Christine intervened:

'Excuse me, but am I to understand that this service to mark the Year of Peace is going to be something of a military occasion, with dignitaries keeping themselves to themselves? If this is about the Year of Peace, could there not be something a bit more inclusive and less formal about the event?

'For example if it's at Westminster Abbey (which I'm sure has a lot of doors) why not have everyone gather outside in the precincts and then have something sung or said that invites people in. That way everyone would be in the procession and it would ensure that people would end up sitting next to folk they didn't necessarily know.'

The Convener responded: 'I don't think that's very practicable.'

Christine: 'Oh yes it is. Two months ago we had over five hundred people gathered outside St Giles' Cathedral in Edinburgh. It was a World Council of Churches event. We taught everyone a freedom song from South Africa in harmony. Then they all walked singing into the cathedral through six different doors and were inside and in their places in under four minutes. If that can happen in Edinburgh, why not in London?'

There was another embarrassed hush.

Convener: 'Young lady, I don't think you understand. When we are talking about this service, we are talking about the Queen of the United Kingdom.'

Christine: 'Sir, and when I am talking about public worship, I am talking about the King of Kings.'

We never heard any more about the service for the Year of Peace.

Nineteen
Foreign tongues

I cannot remember the names of the two brothers. We must have met over twenty years ago, but I sense that Gwyn and Dafydd might not offend them as surrogates. On their father's side they were of Welsh stock, though born in a northern industrial city.

The local Baptist church had a lively youth group which the brothers attended in their teenage years. Thanks to the effective ministry of a well-known evangelist, who was pastor of that church, both boys came to faith, and continued their association with the congregation as long as they lived at home.

Their father was not a religious man. He had long since turned his back on the demanding chapel life in which he was reared in a Welsh valley, but he had no desire to discourage his sons from pursuing their nascent faith.

Eight or so years passed between their conversion and a terminal diagnosis being made of their father. He had inoperable cancer, but faced his impending death with stoicism accompanied by considerable pain. The boys wondered whether it might be helpful if their pastor paid a visit to the dying man. Their dad said he was open to that, so one of the sons arranged for the visit.

The father came from a large family of brothers who rallied round in his last weeks to offer him company and support to his wife. He was never alone, and it was in such circumstances that the pastor visited him. Eventually the man died and the pastor was asked to conduct his funeral.

In the course of time, the same pastor published a short memoir of his life and ministry, a copy of which came into the hands of the sons. On reading it they learned of something which hitherto they had never known. The pastor wrote of how one of the most significant moments in his ministry was when he was asked to come to the bedside of a dying man whose sons had come to faith in the church of which he was minister. As he sought to offer spiritual comfort to the dying man, an amazing thing happened. In response, as it were, to the pastor's ministrations, the dying man was given the gift of tongues and began to praise God in the language of heaven.

When both boys were next at home and in the company of their uncles, they mentioned this amazing event and wondered why they had never been told about it.

'Oh, your dad wasn't speaking in tongues,' insisted one of their uncles. 'He was swearing at that bloody minister in Welsh.'

Twenty
Against the grain

The Special Unit in Barlinnie Prison, Glasgow, was intended for the most untameable of convicts. Ironically its success seems to have led to its closure.

The facility, housed in the former women's prison, had fewer than a dozen men who had all caused mayhem in other establishments. They were looked after by prison staff who had volunteered for the post which required them to forfeit distance and safety. They passed the day alongside the inmates, wore no uniforms and were called by their first names.

I had visited the Unit once before when I was a student, but I asked to visit it again because I wanted to see whether Jimmy Boyle would take a commission for a piece of sculpture.

Jimmy was the Unit's most notorious resident. He was allegedly responsible for at least one murder at a time when violent gangs menaced several areas of the city. When in Peterhead Prison, he had embarked on 'dirty' protests. He was deemed unresponsive and disruptive. But when he and others like him were moved to a place where prisoners were decently treated, exposed to the world of culture, and encouraged to develop latent talents and interests, changes happened. Then Jimmy shone.

It was coming up to the end of my three-year honorary appointment as Rector of the University of Glasgow, and I wanted to give the University a gift a little different from the crystal wine glasses my immediate predecessor had offered. I wanted it to be an artwork which would represent the talent of a transformed individual of innate artistic and intellectual ability. So I wrote to him, knowing that he had done some commissions before, and that he would direct any financial emolument to a charity of his choice. He agreed to meet me.

There was no awkwardness in gaining access to the Special Unit, and on arrival I was introduced to several of the residents.

Jimmy was very warm in his greeting and asked me if I'd like some coffee. He took me to his workroom, a former cell which housed countless chisels, hammers, knives and other items which could harm the body. It was rather surreal being in this confined space with a convicted murderer. But what surprised me more was that Jimmy had a coffee machine with real ground coffee, the smell of which pervaded the immediate environs.

He had a project in mind which he was already working on. It depicted a scene with which I had been familiar from childhood. There were two huddles of small girls each gathered round an older girl ready to play at skipping. Between them was a wire representing the skipping rope; at the rope's centre was a girl springing up in delight and freedom. On its completion, this was the sculpture I presented to the university.

In time Jimmy was released. He got married and lived within and outside Scotland, involved in charitable work. He wrote books and, like other former inmates, never again engaged in criminal activity. In 1994, after successfully rehabilitating these prisoners, the government closed the Special Unit which had been in operation since 1973.

Note: Jimmy's published books include *A Sense of Freedom*, *Pain of Confinement* and *Hero of the Underworld*.

Twenty One
Mothering

Dorothy Robins had lived all her life in the house where she was born, in a small rural town near Detroit, Michigan. She was the youngest of three sisters, and both her siblings, after college and marriage, moved away from their home town. Dorothy never married, but secured a good job in a finance company, lived happily with her parents, and enjoyed spending time with good friends.

Her father died in his mid-sixties, and her mother's health gradually deteriorated thereafter. It wasn't just her body which weakened: her mind soon began to be affected by dementia. Looking after her mother was not a burden to Dorothy, but it was time-consuming. It meant that she couldn't give as much attention to areas of her life which brought her joy and fulfilment.

She was keen that her mum should live at home for as long as possible; but the time came when the doctor advised that – for her mother and for her own good – the old lady would soon need twenty-four-hour assistance which would be better provided in a care facility.

Dorothy looked at several, and eventually found one in a neighbourhood familiar to her mother, where she gradually settled in. Every second day, after work, the dutiful daughter popped in to see her mother, as she also did on Sunday afternoons.

Mental deterioration gradually took its toll, and bewilderment and frustration became increasingly evident in her mother's demeanour. Days passed when there would be no inkling of familiarity with her daughter, or even an answer given when Dorothy asked, 'Mum, do you know who I am?' It seemed that her mother was in a world resistant to any attempts to connect her with normality.

For reasons unknown to her, Dorothy decided one day that it

might be good to take some music to play to her mum. She transferred on to cassette tapes the music of the forties and fifties, the years when her mother had been a teenager. It was not hard to find material, as her mother had amassed a wide range of long-playing records by singers like Patsy Cline, Frank Sinatra, The Andrews Sisters. On the reverse side of the tape, she recorded a selection of hymns which she found on an LP produced by a prestigious Detroit church choir.

Dorothy brought these along with some tray-bakes on the following Sunday afternoon. There was, as anticipated, no recognition of her by her mum; but Dorothy was used to this. She told her mother all her news, made her some coffee, and then suggested that they might like to listen to some music.

She turned on her cassette player and the sounds of post-war popular music filled the room. It was during the third or fourth track that she noticed her mother's feet beginning to twitch in time to the music. And as the tracks continued, her hands, which were usually knotted to each other, unravelled; at times the old lady would sway with the beat.

At the end of the tape, Dorothy played the other side – hymns which she knew her mother, a life-long church member, would have sung in her youth. Hymns such as *'Blessed assurance, Jesus is mine'*, *'What wondrous love is this?'* and *'Come thou font of every blessing'*.

To her astonishment, her mum not only moved in time to the music, but she began to sing word perfect all the hymns with clear fondness and familiarity. Dorothy could scarcely believe it. But what surprised her most was what happened when the music stopped.

Her mother, who seemed permanently chair-bound, stood up, came over to her daughter, put her arms round her and said, 'Oh Dorothy, what mothering you have given me today.'

Twenty Two
Forenames

The first and only time I saw my father weep was when I was five. It was April, a few days after the third of the month. That was the day on which my brothers, David and Donald, were born. For most of their lives the twins believed that they had been called after two family doctors in the practice in which we were registered. But this was not the case, or rather it was only half the case.

The situation in which I saw my father weep was the house of his parents, my grandparents, Tam and Murn Bell. To call it a house would be deceptive. It was what was known as 'a room, kitchen and scullery'. Even that is a misnomer, because the small kitchen and scullery were conjoined. The accommodation was one of four similar in a two-storey tenement block. Each household had a room no more than five metres by four, in which there were two bed recesses. There was also access to shared outside toilets and a washhouse. It was in such a place that my grandparents reared two sons, and for a time two nieces while their mother was in a psychiatric hospital.

On the day in question, my father sat with my grandparents around their dining table. I was on the floor playing with toys when I heard the sound of convulsive weeping from the three of them. I still feel haunted by it when I remember the occasion. The reason for the weeping was the naming of the twins as David and Donald.

At that time, a custom to which some families subscribed was to give the firstborn son the Christian name or names of his maternal grandfather. Hence I was called John Lamberton Bell. The second son would then be called after the paternal grandfather, which should have meant that David, the elder twin, would have been called Thomas Bell after Tam.. But there was, or had been, another Thomas Bell.

He was my father's younger brother, by all accounts a very lively, cocky, adventurous and affectionate teenager who played the piano accordion, was forever getting into scrapes, and had the notion that when he grew up he might become either a policeman or a minister. Tom was also a diabetic, and at the early age of fifteen died in hospital from pneumonia.

It was a grief which induced in Murn, my very resilient grandmother, a psychological breakdown. And it hurt the heart of Tam, my hard-working communist grandfather, so much that – until his death thirty years later – Tom was one of two deceased relatives about whom he could scarcely speak without shedding tears. The other was his brother Jock who was killed during the First World War in Palestine.

Tom died four years before the twins were born. Hence my father and mother instinctively felt that to have one twin bearing the same name as his deceased uncle might incur awkwardness or a special favouring as regards his relationship with his grandparents.

So the decision was made to call the older twin David Robertson, after his paternal great-grandfather, and the younger Donald McLaughlan after their own doctor who had been particularly helpful in identifying cancer in my mother's mother, something her own physician had failed to recognise.

It was an act of both pain and kindness for my father to make that decision, but it enabled unbiased affection to be shown to the twins by Tam and Murn, their proud grandparents.

Twenty Three
The T shirt

Greenbelt Festival is an annual event which has had a major impact on my and my colleagues' lives. Starting as a Christian arts festival in a field, and favoured mostly by the evangelical constituency in the beginning, it has expanded in scope, in political and social interest, in theological breadth and in its appeal to persons within and outside Christian communities.

Our initial engagement was to provide morning worship alongside an array of noted expositors who led Bible studies, first thing in the morning, in a range of tented locations. We noticed that little by way of worship happened at night, so we suggested that we might offer this, on the basis that celebrating God in the darkness has a different ambience than in the morning light.

The first time we led late-night worship, we were the victims of some innocent energy-saver who turned off our lights from a central control and left us in dark. On subsequent nights people came armed with torches and in future years sympathetic worshippers drove their cars to face towards the tent in which we gathered, so that in the event of a power cut, their headlights would lighten our darkness.

Over the years we were the sole agency offering late-night worship and would often attract large crowds crammed into substantial marquees. We were committed to maximising congregational engagement, by shared extempore prayer, biblical conversations, and *a capella* singing of songs from our own stable and from elsewhere in the world. Such services could be intensely moving and immensely funny. They were times of rich blessing.

None more so, perhaps, than the Sunday evening service which was often devoted to the ministry of healing. We had a range of suitable songs, and always chose one of Jesus' miracles for shared reflection. Towards the end, we invited people, if they wished, to come towards the podium area where the worship leaders stood. It was often decorated with bright cloths and branches. There people could light a candle and place it alongside others in token of their concern for those who were ill, bereft or confused.

We also had an area where people who wished personal prayer could kneel down as one or two leaders slowly walked from one person to another, laying hands on the bowed head and offering prayer.

The atmosphere was always hushed, always reverent. People were told that, if they wished, they could stay in the marquee after the service. The main lights were dimmed, and only the candles remained. Sometimes worshippers would stay sitting in silence for up to an hour.

On one particular occasion, my colleague Graham and I stayed behind to extinguish lit candles and tidy up the tent after people had left. He noticed that there was a woman, who had been at worship, pacing up and down outside the marquee There seemed no purpose to her movement, although occasionally she would glance over to where we were sitting. It puzzled Graham sufficiently that he slowly walked over to the woman and began a conversation. It lasted around ten minutes, after which she went away and he reflected on their meeting:

'I asked her if there was something she wanted to say, or any help that she was looking for. She replied with a litany of complaints: her marriage was breaking up; her children had turned against their mother; she was both unhappy and unpopular at her work. But everything would be OK, because "Jesus was her Saviour".

'I noticed that she was wearing a T-shirt, on which was emblazoned the slogan "Jesus is the answer". I suggested to her that Jesus had never said that, and she was quite shocked by my comment.

'So then I said to her, "Jesus may be your saviour, but he never said he was the answer. He did say, 'I am the Way.' Faith is not about a destination, it's about a journey on which standing still is not an option.'

She had never thought of that.

Twenty Four
The benefactor

For almost five years and at sporadic intervals, I received a posted letter in which there was nothing more than a five pound note and a notelet which had an image of a bunch of white heather tied with a red tartan bow. On it was written these words:

God willing, this will help your work.

I had no idea who sent it; nor was there ever any indication on the stamp of its place of origin, though the writing suggested that it might be an elderly person.

I remembered an old friend of mine, who from time to time had been the recipient of vitriolic correspondence, saying, 'Son, if you ever get an anonymous letter, don't read it. If you do, and it's critical of you, you might just change something and that will let the sender know that he or she has had the desired effect and they may then become controlling.' But these were not critical letters from someone too cowardly to be identified. These were notes from a benefactor.

It would be in the fourth year that one day when I was visiting my grandmother she said, 'There's an odd thing that's happening to me. From time to time, somebody from a local shop arrives at my door with either a bowl of fruit or a bunch of flowers, but refuses to say who is sending them.' 'Have you any idea who it is?' I asked. 'No,' she replied, 'but I'm going to find out.'

The next time the delivery girl came, my grannie said that she would refuse to accept any more fruit or flowers unless the sender was identified. The girl told her, 'I shouldn't be telling you this, Mrs Bell, but it's Annie Sampson.' This was a lady whom I had never met, but who lived about a hundred yards from my grandmother. My grannie, who was then ninety, said that Annie was about fifteen years younger than her, but had bad health which saw her taken into hospital every so often for respite care. I told the story of the anonymous letters I had been receiving, and we concurred that the source might be the same as for the fruit and flowers.

So I rang Annie and introduced myself, at which point she said, 'Oh, so you've found out.' I arranged to visit her, and subsequently entered a fairly frugal household with a delightful frail but kindly inhabitant. She had been widowed for some time, had a son who lived in a neighbouring town, and was clearly limited in her mobility. She was not a well woman, but we had a lovely conversation in which I discovered that she was Roman Catholic, but regretted that she was often unable to attend Mass. I thanked her for her kindness and told her the purposes to which I had put her gifts.

A year later, I had a call from the parish priest at St Joseph's R.C. church in Kilmarnock. He had phoned to say that Annie had died and he wondered whether I might give a short tribute at her funeral. I said I would be very privileged to do so, and he indicated that I was free to suggest an appropriate scripture reading. I chose Mark 12, verses 41-44. This is the passage which refers to how Jesus noticed rich men priding themselves in their largesse at the offering bowl in the temple. In contrast a poor widow came and dropped in two tiny coins. Jesus praised her generosity, because whereas the men gave of their disposable surplus, she gave of her capital.

I didn't say much by the way of a tribute. I didn't know Annie or her family or her history sufficiently well. But I had decided to refer to the way my grannie and I had benefited from her kindness. So I began, after the Gospel reading, by saying, 'Friends, when we met Annie Sampson, we met this poor widow.'

At the end of the service, a number of people came over to me and said, 'She sent flowers to my mother as well.' And I realised why one of Luke's beatitudes says simply: Blessed are the poor.

They know how to be generous.

Twenty Five
Released from bondage

An email from Joshua Harvey indicated that we had never met, but he was hoping that I might be able to help him. He was coming to Glasgow to enrol in a postgraduate course in musical theatre at the Conservatoire. It seemed to him that on top of his fees and living expenses, the cost of a place in a student residence was almost prohibitive. He wondered if I knew of an alternative, cheaper situation.

As it happened, I had a spare room in my large flat and had had lodgers before. So I offered it to him for whatever seemed a manageable amount. After sealing the deal, he indicated that he might be getting married and wondered whether, if that happened, he could bring his wife. I wrote back saying that getting married should not be dependent on my willingness to have a newly-wed couple in my house; he had to make up his own mind. He did. They got married and they came to Glasgow – he a 33-year-old church musician and junior college lecturer; she a 22-year-old undergraduate at a Mormon college.

Ashley looked and acted like the archetypal sweet American gal, keenly minding her Ps and Qs and avidly devoted to her husband's happiness. When she set up in the kitchen, it was with a laptop opened at a cookery website, the rules of which she followed exactly, producing a range of evening meals without ever remembering exactly what she had done.

She called me Sir for the first two weeks until I persuaded her that as we were living in close proximity, John would be much easier on my ears. I discovered that in her Mormon university, behavioural regulations were strictly enforced. If you were caught holding hands with someone of the opposite sex, there was a $10 fine; the same for smelling of smoked tobacco, rising to $15 if there was alcohol on your breath. I reckoned that many of the undergraduates I had known would probably be bankrupt within a week.

She had almost completed her course, but needed two more credits which could be obtained if she enrolled in a reputable college course in Glasgow. She looked around for an appropriate establishment and found suitable courses. One day after a month's tuition, I asked her, 'How are you getting on in your music classes, Ashley?'

'Well,' she said, 'not all the kids understand me, and I don't understand all of them. But that'll happen. It's performance-based, so we do a lot together.'

'And what about your lecturers?' She replied, 'One or two of them are a bit dull. But there's one guy who is superb. I'm sure I'll learn a lot in his class. But you know, the other day I heard him say the F word.'

'Oh Ashley,' I replied solicitously, 'and what did you think when you heard him saying the F word?'

'I just said, "Thank you, Jesus,"' she replied.

In time this liberated young woman helped Josh lead music in the Jesuit church in Glasgow and, at the vigil Mass on the eve of Easter, I was present to see her baptised as a Christian and received into the Church.

They now live in Missouri, still very happily married with three lovely children so far.

Twenty Six
Telling it

I did not know Megan very well. I was present at her wedding and three years later I scattered her ashes. But she remains in my mind as one of the finest, most honest and perceptive young women I ever met.

I had asked her to come up to the Youth Camp on Iona for a couple of days, during which she had agreed to lead a seminar on disability. She herself was disabled. She had had polio as a child and the signs would never be erased. One side of her body was clearly compromised, she walked with a limp and her speech, though clear, had been impaired in quality,

Around forty teenagers were having lunch when she arrived. I had not advertised her in advance, and it was interesting to see a sense of uneasiness on some of their faces when she hobbled along the dining room looking for a place to sit.

Later in the afternoon, the group gathered and I introduced Megan to them stating the obvious, namely that polio had affected her from childhood. Therefore she lived with a permanent disability. I then asked her to speak to the group.

She began by saying forcefully:

'The first thing I want to say about disabled people is that some of them are ugly.'

This was not at all what I had anticipated. And then she said,

'Some of them have ugly manners, some of them have ugly tempers, some of them have ugly attitudes, and some of them make themselves look ugly. And if you don't think disabled people can be ugly, then you're patronising them.'

It was an electric beginning to a magnificently liberating session – liberating in that it freed people from their apprehensions and their presumptions regarding people who were not able-bodied.

And only someone as disabled as Megan could tell it as it really is.

Twenty Seven
The reel thing

Even though he is now dead, I will not name him. But perhaps from heaven he might smile on what happened a long time ago when he was an apprentice in the service of the Lord, and zealous – as some apprentices are – to do something different and make an impact.

The issue was Remembrance Sunday, an event which annually saw the church packed to capacity. The uniformed children's organisations would be there as well as a contingent of army cadets. People who never came to church would arrive bringing their grief, their widowhood, their unrequited anger. Others would come (in the days before white poppies) deliberately not wearing a red poppy, as an alternative symbolic action. And some people who were always at church would be absent.

He had never led the Remembrance Sunday service before. He knew the congregation would be disappointed that it was he, the junior, the substitute, in charge rather than the incumbent; but maybe some would be sympathetic.

In other churches the two-minute silence ended with a trumpet or bugle call. This congregation did not have access to such instrumental music. But being Scots, those of a certain vintage would know the bagpipe lament *The Floo'ers o' the Forest*.

In the absence of a bagpiper, he decided that the next best thing would be to play a cassette recording of that solemn tribute to the dead of the Battle of Flodden after two minutes in the absence of sound. And he found, on a tape of miscellaneous Scottish music, that very lament. So he placed it in the cassette player, plugged it into the pulpit, and just before the service played the short piece right through to check that all was well.

The building began to fill as the solemn adults and solemnised children on their best behaviour filed in. At ten to eleven, he entered the church, called the people to worship and they sang Psalm 124 as was the tradition.

Now Israel may say and that truly,
'If that the Lord had not been on our side' ...

He had a prayer prepared with three optional endings. One would be chosen depending on how long the call to worship, the psalm and the sitting and standing had encroached on the time before the eleventh hour struck.

He asked the congregation to stand, he called them to remembrance, and for two minutes all was quiet.

Carefully he pressed the play button on the cassette recorder. In a few seconds the sound emanated throughout the building of Jimmy Shand and his band playing *The Gay Gordons*.

He had forgotten to rewind the tape.

Twenty Eight

Tears

The English Reformed Church in Amsterdam has always had a very mixed congregation in terms of racial profile. The 14th-century building occupied by the congregation was originally the chapel for a settlement of charitable women called *Begijntjes* in Dutch or *Beguines* in French. After the Reformation, the Amsterdam civic authorities, knowing that their prosperity depended on trade, gave over the building for worship in the English language, primarily for the convenience of merchants and visitors from Britain.

Now it is a community in which most of the members are either residents or visitors whose second language is English. Vito was the name of a man in his early twenties who was a regular attender when I was associate pastor there. What drew him to my attention was both that he was clearly a foreign national, and that at the end of worship he would often sit in the church in tears.

I never learned his name until I asked him one Sunday whether he would like to join the church's International Club, a weekly gathering of around thirty young people in their late teens and twenties. He agreed to come, and soon everyone who welcomed him became clearly endeared to him. We learned that he was Filipino, but he said little more about himself except that he missed being with his family.

It took me the best part of three months to win his confidence sufficient to have him agree to meet me alone for coffee. We did this several times. The conversation never got very far, and I sensed that the reason was not simply that English was his third language. Something which intrigued me was that whenever we met, we seemed to walk furtively through the narrow streets of the city, with Vito constantly looking over his shoulder or suddenly changing our direction of travel.

Eventually the truth came out.

He had been in the Philippine navy during the Marcos dictatorship. He hated Marcos and he hated the navy; so he jumped ship when his vessel docked in Amsterdam. But he did not immediately seek political asylum. Instead he bummed around, doing odd jobs, and living with other illegal immigrants until he managed to get a place of his own.

One day he was approached by a person who offered him a job transporting goods from the French Mediterranean seaboard to Amsterdam. The pay was attractive, so he took it, and discovered soon after that he was being employed as a runner for a Chinese drug triad who favoured Filipino drivers. They did not look Chinese, and would not discolour through blushing if interrogated.

It had been made clear to him that he was now tightly in the control of the triad. If he stopped working for them, they indicated they would make it known to the police that he was an illegal immigrant; if he handed himself over to the police, he would be exported to his native land and any punishment to which the navy might sentence him for desertion.

I asked him why it was that at the end of Sunday services, he sat with tears in his eyes. He replied, 'It is because the church is the only place I can go to where I remember that life is meant to be good.'

Twenty Nine
Making it easy for others

When George MacLeod of the Iona Community was eighty-eight, his health took a temporary turn for the worse, and he was laid up in bed in the Founder's Room in the Abbey. On the basis that we were 'old friends' – an accolade I found quite unusual since not long before he had berated me regarding my dress sense – he asked if I would deliver meals to his room, 'along with a chocolate biscuit if you can find one'.

After a few days, he felt better and decided to head back to his home in Edinburgh. I said that I would accompany him and arranged for Chris Hoon, one of our youth volunteers, to drive a car up to the harbour at Oban so that we could comfortably transport George to his destination.

That day, there was an exceptionally high tide, so much so that when we crossed in the ferry from Mull to the mainland, the ship sat so high above the pier that the long gangplank – by which foot passengers had to alight – was almost vertical. I could see the apprehension in George's eyes and was sure that, being slightly shaky on his legs, he would not want to walk down.

He handed me his case and asked me to go in front of him. Then he stepped on to the gangplank, sat down, and for the next seven or eight minutes inched himself down on his backside. There were between eighty and a hundred people waiting to get on the boat, who witnessed this slow disembarkation.

I felt humiliated for George that he, who had commanded soldiers, addressed academic and ecclesiastical assemblies, and been harangued by his own denomination for relentlessly encouraging the Church to denounce the possession of nuclear arms, should be reduced to this ungainly exit.

He eventually reached the bottom of the gangplank. I helped him to his feet and took him over to the car and our driver, who was looking a little nervous at meeting such a distinguished person.

I said, 'Lord MacLeod, this is Chris Hoon. He's driving us to Glasgow.' Then completely oblivious to what had just transpired, but keen to endear himself to his slightly apprehensive chauffeur, he said with confidence and charm:

'I am George MacLeod and I'm very pleased to meet you.

'Now, tell me, are you a Christian or a Presbyterian?'

Thirty

Betty

Betty Logan was a hairdresser. She had a small salon in an old housing area. She was married to George who had been a childhood friend of my father, and they had two sons. I suppose in one way or another I had known her since I was a toddler, although we never spoke directly to each other till I was in my fifties.

That occasion was when I had been asked to preach in St Kentigern's Church, a modern building in a social housing scheme in Kilmarnock. At that time to 'preach' involved doing everything else – talk to the kids, introduce the hymns, read the Bible, give the announcements and deliver the sermon.

Though I had been preaching for over twenty-five years, I always prepared a new sermon and at least the first prayer. Sometimes I would lead the second prayer, the intercessions, extempore: i.e. without notes. Which is what I did on this particular Sunday.

I always tried to avoid cliches in prayers, such as 'beds of sickness' or 'travelling mercies'. But there was one phrase which occasionally I would use. I first heard it one evening at the service of prayers for healing in Iona Abbey. I have no idea where it comes from, but I find the words very poignant:

> 'We pray for those who at night cry,
> "I wish to God it were morning"
> and, come morning, cry,
> "I wish to God it were night."'

I must have used these words that day, because after the service, as I was greeting people at the door, this small, shrivelled, troubled-looking woman in her late sixties caught a hold of my stole, pulled me down to her level, and said, 'How did you know?'

'How did I know what, Betty?' I asked.

'How did you know that at night I cry "I wish to God it were morning"?'

I had no answer. I was stunned and moved, but I mumbled something and then said, 'God bless you, Betty.'

Later in the day, I learned from my mother that Betty's marriage had broken up, and that for a long time she had been a severe alcoholic. Ten years later I met her son whom I had not seen since high school. Subsequently, when we were talking about his mother, I learned that Betty had been off the drink for ten years, and that she began the journey to sobriety around the time when we met in St Kentigern's.

Thirty One

The tug

In Glasgow there was a large church which could accommodate over a thousand people. Whether it ever regularly held that many is a matter of doubt. It was, to some extent, a monument to the inability of Presbyterians to get on with each other. Like other Victorian edifices it was raised as a result of the Church of Scotland splitting in two in 1843 over the issue of patronage.

All over the country, those who were favourable or at least not hostile to the local landlord (who often paid for the minister and maintained the property) stayed in the 'parish' church. Those who preferred a more independent polity favoured the break-away 'free' kirk. Its buildings were sometimes financed by a person of substantial wealth and influence, but more often the new church was paid for by local subscription. Often the new edifice would boast a larger gallery, a higher tower or some other noticeable feature with which the older parish church could not compete.

After reunification of the warring tribes in 1927, there was no attempt to reduce the number of buildings. In my home town, there was the Old High Parish Church and the West High Church both within the reconstituted Church of Scotland and a hundred yards apart. But even until the end of the 20th century neither would have much to do with the other. Indifference still reigned.

As the heyday of church growth in the fifties waned, so congregations grew smaller. In the largest of the buildings most worshippers, rather than sit together, positioned themselves in splendid isolation, occupying their family pews with ever-shrinking families. When I began attending the church with a thousand seats, it had around forty regulars who located themselves like the Jewish diaspora in different spots. It was the Body of Christ with acne.

However a new incumbent was not cowed by a building which proclaimed it had the second slimmest steeple in Europe, the highest pulpit steps in Scotland, and the most prestigious 20th-century stained-glass windows in Glasgow. He invested in blue cord and corralled the flock into the front six rows on either side of the central aisle. In no time at all the singing improved, people greeted each other as they came and went, and shared leadership ensured that more than the preacher's voice was heard.

There was a family who, in the new configuration, usually sat near the front and on the right of the central aisle. They were a mother, father and three-year-old son called Matthew. The child was a beautiful blond-haired, blue-eyed boy with a ruddy complexion. Like other children who have Down's syndrome, Matthew loved colours and people. Every pullover he wore caught the eye, and every person he met was presumed to be a friend.

On one particular Sunday I was located one row behind them. While Matthew's parents were greeting someone who had just sat beside them, he was preoccupied with the bald pate of a certain Mr Sinclair, an austere and rather censorious Presbyterian elder.

What particularly fascinated Matthew was the crescent of longish grey hair surrounding the bald top of Sinclair's head. I watched as he leaned forward as if to pull the locks and then withdrew. I wondered if I should alert his parents regarding his possible intentions, but decided to wait and see if anything happened. It did.

He began to tug slightly on Mr Sinclair's grey outcrop; as he did, old Sinclair's head tilted back. It happened half a dozen times. I was sure that the ancient of days would turn round and admonish the parents to control their child. He was that kind of man.

When he eventually did turn round, his face was met with the smiling visage of a three-year-old, who pointing to his own chest said, 'Matthew.' In response to this, I was astounded to hear Mr Sinclair point to himself and say, 'Eh ... George.' That was the first time I learned the man's forename, and it was a three-year-old child who had elicited the information.

Matthew was an angel of mercy, who not only helped that congregation to integrate, but also enabled them to lose their fear of those who looked or sounded different.

Thirty Two
Times! Citizen!

Most towns with a population of between ten and twenty thousand are places where the majority of the inhabitants would be able to recognise – if not know at least a little about – the 'worthies', citizens who were renowned for eccentricities in their dress, speech or behaviour.

My grandparents grew up in different corners of Kilmarnock at the turn of the nineteenth century. Between them they would share tales of past worthies with exotic names such as 'Jingle the Keys' or 'Martha Pouf' or 'Wullie Hats'. These people were often vagrants or street traders, each with their personalised vocabulary and mannerisms.

Even when the town grew to fifty thousand, the worthies were still almost universally known. One such was Wee Boabbie Clearie, a diminutive man who wandered the back streets in the morning with a wooden barrow. From the rubbish piled up outside their shops by grocers and fruiterers, he would extract wooden boxes which could be broken down into firewood for kindling. When he had sufficient, he would roam through streets known to him, where women like my grandmother would give him sixpence or a shilling for these wares.

There was a man called John Foy, formerly a soldier, who exhibited post-traumatic stress disorder before that term had been coined. He had gone into the Second World War cogent and able, but was discharged as someone haunted by his army experience and unsuited to steady work. He often sat in the town centre, sometimes inebriated, but always willing to talk to anyone. When a man of substance walked past him, John would shout, 'Hello Major!' and if Major made no response, John would assail him with colourful, derogatory language.

There was Piebald Lindsay, who had a greater degree of sophistication than the others. He was a rag and bone merchant, whose horse-drawn open trailer rattled through the streets of town while he, as the mood took him, blasted a few notes on a bashed trumpet and shouted, 'Toys for rags; money for rags.'

Hearing this good news, children would pester their parents for old jerseys, pullovers, cardigans, jeans and shirts which might be exchanged for a few pence or a plastic novelty. Often this quest resulted in disappointment when the child, innocent of textiles, was told by Piebald that garments made partly or wholly of nylon or some other humanly fabricated cloth were worthless.

And there was Wee Oddie.

This was another diminutive man, whose frame was disfigured probably as a result of right hemiplegia (a stroke) which weakened and restricted movement on the left-hand side of his body. He limped to the left, his left arm hung virtually lifeless, and his speech too was compromised. But people knew his voice, because from the publication of the afternoon newspapers at around 4.30pm and for the next two-and-a-half hours, Oddie would sit in a doorway beside a pub at the junction of St Marnock's Street and King Street.

The two newspapers would be held under his left armpit as he shouted, 'Times! Citizen!' with the emphasis on the last syllable of the second paper. When people approached they would state the newspaper they wanted. He would fish it out of his bundle with his right hand, take their money and – if change were needed – find that in his right-hand pocket.

I don't know whether he was christened Duncan or James, Alex or Fergus. He was, to everyone, 'Wee Oddie', a child of God, known not for his potential but – sadly – usually remembered for his problem.

Thirty Three
The mother of many

Unless you are a North American Mennonite involved in church music, you are unlikely to know the name of Mary Oyer, born in 1913.

She was a remarkable woman, an ethno-musicologist in her own right before the term was popularised. A skilled cellist of the traditional classical variety, she earned a doctorate in musical arts at the University of Ann Arbor. She held professorships in the USA and Taiwan, where she became increasingly open to the musical genres of other cultures. She spoke of once in Asia being shown a stringed instrument which bore no resemblance to anything she had seen before. And yet within minutes she was able to play a recognisable tune on it.

She was renowned for her effective college teaching, encouraging students to expand their horizons while expecting diligence in academic study. 'Firm but friendly' would probably describe her demeanour as a professor.

She also had a passion for congregational song, something which is inbred in many Mennonites, whose early immigrant churches disparaged instrumental accompaniment in favour of four-part congregational singing. This denomination, more than any other, knows the value, the enjoyment and the spiritual benefits of singing together.

Mary lived to a good old age. She never married, and retained what one might call an archetypal American settler demeanour – no showiness in dress, no vulgarity in language, no indulgences which inhibit clear thinking; but a wealth of wisdom, knowledge, reminiscences, politeness and gentle humour.

One year, when she was well beyond the time of retirement, she attended a weekend conference of Mennonite musicians in

North Virginia. During the closing act of worship, Psalm 113 was read, after which the conference organiser, a distinguished Mennonite professor of music, spoke.

He began by asking those who had ever been taught by Mary Oyer to stand. He asked those who had taught alongside Mary Oyer to stand. He then asked those who had been participants in workshops she had led to stand. By this time, there was no one left sitting apart from Mary.

Then, with winsome delicacy, he referred to the closing verse of Psalm 113:

> God makes the woman in a childless house
> a happy mother of children.

And speaking directly to Mary, he said,

> 'Look around you, Mary.
> These are the children you have mothered.
> And we are all profoundly grateful.'

Thirty Four
Good Friday

Given his slight frame, unassuming manner and gentle voice, Nestor did not seem like someone who would rock the boat. So when he mentioned the term 'ambush liturgy', it sounded both out of kilter with conventional language for worship, and something which one would not immediately associate with such a pleasant young man.

The term emerged in the Philippines during the years of popular discontent which was one of the hallmarks of the Marcos regime. It referred to small groups of religious 'activists' who would beat a drum in a public space to attract attention. Once a crowd had gathered, someone would recount to the listeners a story or saying of Jesus, and then, drawing on the biblical text, indicate in clear terms how the will of God and the will of the regime were at odds with each other.

This might be followed by a song or a prayer. And at any time the *ad hoc* assembly might be dissolved and the people scattered if lookouts indicated the approach of members of the police force or army. But a more memorable liturgical practice which Nestor spoke about was what happened in his small rural Baptist church on Good Friday.

The congregation would gather early in the morning and sit or stand round a large Western* crucifix with a figure of a European Jesus nailed to the oak or teak cross. After a short prayer and Gospel reading appropriate to the day, one or two people would begin to destroy the crucifix, smashing the figure and breaking the wood until it was in pieces.

The women would then go and gather rags while the men went to gather bamboo stalks. The latter, using native wood, would fashion a bamboo cross: the women, using discarded clothing would fashion a rag-doll Jesus. The figure would then be affixed to the cross, and the cross made to stand upright.

Then there would be more readings, prayers and songs as the small congregation remembered the death of Jesus.

When asked the reason for what seemed like a rather irreverent act of public devotion, Nestor replied:

'We do this because we believe that Jesus will only be able to liberate Filipino people if we liberate Jesus from being a Western idol.'

---

* *There would be little difficulty in finding such an object. Religious life in the Philippines was percolated with Western artefacts and assumptions at that time. For example, until relatively recently, the hymnal used in the Philippines Episcopal Church was an import of that used in the Episcopal Church of the USA.*

Thirty Five
Isaiah

She was standing in an alcove of the long corridor which joined the chapel to the main house, and she was softly weeping.

I wasn't sure what to do, so I just stood close enough to her to make her aware that I was there. After a minute or two, she turned towards me and said, 'I'm not crying because there's something wrong. It's actually because it's all right now.'

I asked her if she wanted to talk about it, and she said, 'Yes. We'll probably never see each other again. Let's sit down somewhere.'

So we did, and this was her story:

'I have always been a believer. More so since I was a teenager and I had a strong sense of the presence of Jesus in my life. And I've always read the Bible and prayed.

'But I've also been dealing with something which will probably never go away. You see, after my mother died, when I was eight, my father started sexually abusing me. This went on until I was about fourteen, and I went to live with an aunt. I've had very good counselling which has enabled me to put these past dire experiences behind me.

'I work in the city. I do shift work, which means sometimes I'm not able to go to church on Sunday mornings. But I always manage Sunday evenings. I love it, especially in the winter when it's dark and cold outside, and it's warm and bright in the church. I love just sitting before the service and looking at the two candles lit on the communion table.

'We have a new minister. He's a lovely man, so is his wife. They're still young and they have two children. Sometimes I babysit for them.

'The thing is that sometimes at the evening service the minister will begin his payers by saying, "Now let's all close our eyes, and feel our Father's loving arms surrounding us and pulling us close to his presence." I know that God is not like an abusive father, but my body has a memory, and these words tend to bring to mind all that awful stuff in the past.

'But something happened this morning. It was in the chapel. We were singing a hymn which I did not know. It says it is based on words from the prophecy of Isaiah. It was this verse that affected me:

> God says, 'See how a woman cares.
> Shall she forget the child she bore?
> Even if she does, I shan't forget;
> though you feel lost, I'll love you more.*

'I never knew that God was ever referred to in the feminine, as a mother. And now, for the first time probably since I was eight, I feel as if I can embrace God and let God embrace me.

'So ... it's all right now.'

*Isaiah 49:15

Thirty Six
The gift

Half an hour after I checked in at the hotel I had booked in Ho Chi Minh City, I was seated in a nearby park, reading a novel I had started while waiting on my flight from Singapore to Vietnam.

I looked up to find myself surrounded by three young men aged between eighteen and twenty who seemed a little reticent to disturb me. Eventually one said, 'Can we speak to you?'

'Yes,' I replied.

'In English?'

'I will try very hard.'

They then explained that, for their own advancement, they needed to learn English. They all attended the same night class but there were no books, only lined jotters on which they wrote down words. They had been told that the best way to learn was to engage in conversation with a native speaker. Hence their request.

Having been in the country for less than an hour, I was hesitant as to how I should proceed. So I said, 'If you are serious about speaking English, meet me here in two days (Monday) at the same time (4.30pm). If you will take me to a genuine Vietnamese restaurant – not a tourist one – I will pay for a meal for all of us, and we can speak in English for as long as you want.'

On the Monday, they were all back on time and took me to an area normally forbidden to foreign visitors. I had been informed of a particular Vietnamese delicacy by my colleague in Singapore, so when they asked what I would like to eat, I said, 'Anything but monkey brains.'

They ordered a fish dish, and since two of them worked in catering, they negotiated with the waiting staff for the substantial fish and accompanying vegetables to be cooked in a tureen on the table. It was delicious food, very reasonably priced, and the cooking procedures opened up various avenues of conversation.

They were keen to meet again; that happened twice more during my stay. On the final occasion, they were insistent that I should eat some street food, and do so at the other end of the park in which we had first met, where there was a variety of food stalls and entertainments nearby.

Two of the boys went to buy the food while the third, a slender youth with a very interesting face, sat with me. After a few minutes he said, 'Would you sing me a song from your country?' With the exception of leading a chorus of *Auld Lang Syne*, I had never been asked that before. But I said I would, and told him that the song I was going to sing, *Ae Fond Kiss*, was one which my mother and father often sang to each other.

When I finished, I asked him, 'Would you sing me a song from your country?'

He assented as if it were the most natural thing to do, and told me that the song was one he had learned from his grandparents who were peasant farmers on the Mekong Delta.

And then he began to sing. He had the most beautiful, expressive, light tenor voice. I was deeply moved. He was giving me what no one else could give – the song of his nation through the sound of his voice with no one else in the audience apart from myself. Indeed I felt then and still feel that this was a holy moment, an epiphany never to be repeated.

Thirty Seven
Baby care

The town of Kilmarnock, from which I come, is not a place where self-promotion of either the locality or its citizenry was encouraged. Indeed it might be said that low self-esteem ran through the town as a permanent contagion. In Australia, anyone at risk of having an inflated ego can find themselves the victim of the 'tall poppy syndrome'. They will be cut down, brought low by the censure of others. The equivalent in Kilmarnock is a colloquial phrase of dubious origin which refers to an individual perceived to be acting above their station as 'fancying their barrow'. Such people, like their antipodean counterparts, often find themselves deflated by a carefully worded put-down.

Kilmarnock now – as distinct from the past – has sadly little in which pride could be taken. In the immediate post-war era and until the seventies, it had six major exporting industries which manufactured *inter alia* shoes, carpets, railway engines and hydraulic engineering equipment. The most universally famous export was Johnny Walker's whisky which began flowing from the town in 1860 and continued until, like the other exporting industries, its existence in Kilmarnock was terminated by design of a multinational company with no loyalty to the place or people.

Because the bonded warehouses in which the whisky matured were situated in the town centre, the smell pervaded all nearby precincts including those of the oldest standing structure. This was, and still is, the tower of the Laigh Kirk (Scots for Low Church) – a geographical allusion rather than anything to do with liturgy. The tower bears a plaque dated 1410. The dissent which permeated Presbyterian Scotland in the 18th century regarding patronage was demonstrably present in the very building to which the tower is attached. On July 7th 1763, the congregation made visible objection to the installation of a minister called William

Lindsay who was the preferred candidate chosen by the feudal superior, the Earl of Glencairn.

The streets around the church were full of objectors pelting those favourable to Mr Lindsay with 'filthy substances' according to the chronicler of events. That was outside the building. Inside was not much better. The same chronicler reports how within the sanctuary the affray continued.

> The precentor, William Steven, had his wig tossed in the air, and the Earl of Glencairn was struck on the cheek with a dead cat.*

It was in this church in 2014 that I was invited to preach on the occasion of an anniversary celebration. I felt slightly apprehensive, never having preached in the building before, and aware that there might be some in the congregation who would have known me in a much less formal setting in my youth.

The minister welcomed me warmly, the music was good, the congregation sang well and at the conclusion of the service I went to the door to bid goodbye to everyone. I realised that few people present would have known me. I had left the town over forty years previously, and since then it had become something of a dormitory for those who worked in Glasgow and took advantage of a recently opened motorway connection.

Towards the end of the farewells a woman whom I vaguely recognised approached me, gripped me with her right hand and did not let go. Then, with her index finger, she jabbed me in the chest while uttering the words, 'I used to bath you.' This was her only greeting. She disappeared before I was able to say, 'Time you did it again, sister.' Clearly her words were meant to ensure that I did not fancy my barrow.

* Quoted from *The History of Kilmarnock* by Alexander McKay, 1909 edition, Kilmarnock Standard Printing Works.

Thirty Eight
Free at last

Vikki Andriessen was a woman not easily forgotten. Unaware of her effect on others, she could command a room just by walking into it. It was not that she was tall and uniformed: it was more that she had the kind of face which seemed so determined to say something, that you felt obliged to give her a hearing. But when she spoke, she rarely said anything of world-shattering importance. No, her words were forceful, and often of exaggerated complaint (which is a very Dutch trait) or effusive encouragement.

When she came to church, it was always with Ben, her white-haired, submissive husband. They would always be last in, and would always make for the front row. And, especially in the summer months, Vikki would wear vibrant apparel – a flame red chiffon shift, or a large-patterned print dress with clashing colours. People were wont to say of her, 'She wears clothes better suited to a younger woman.'

After Ben died, she continued to come, though less frequently. On my annual visits covering while the minister was on holiday, she would appear as brightly clad as ever, and would be among the first to leave the building at the end of the service. When I was positioned outside in the courtyard to greet the congregation as they left, Vikki would burst into view, kiss me three times and then exclaim aloud, 'Oh John, how much we miss you. It's because we love you so much. We really do.' She would repeat this, then kiss and hug me before striding off. This left hapless congregants behind her wondering whether they too had to repeat the procedure.

I had not seen her for perhaps ten years when, during one of my short stays, there was a phone call from her, asking whether I might visit her in her home. I was slightly apprehensive, but felt that, given her age, seduction was unlikely. So I went.

It was not the vivacious Vikki I met, but a much diminished older woman clad in her dressing gown, looking worn and tired. We had tea together, and she spoke a bit about her family and her neighbourhood before dealing with the *res ipsa*. She had not been well for a long time, but only recently had been given a diagnosis that she had cancer. It was an incurable but slow cancer, with the expectation that she had another five years to live. I sympathised with having to deal with that kind of information.

And then she said, 'John, I am going to ask you a question to which I want you to answer with great honesty.' I said I would and she continued, 'I want to ask you if God forgives, if God really forgives.' I told her that I believed that absolutely. I assured her that whenever we, in all honesty, admit to what has gone wrong in our lives, and place ourselves at the mercy of God, forgiveness is granted us.

Other details of the conversation need not be shared. After we had spoken, I prayed with her, and soon afterwards I rose to put on my coat and bade her goodbye.

'One other thing, before you go,' she said. 'I'm going to die sometime, and I would like you to take my funeral. Will you?' 'Vikki,' I replied, 'I could be dead before you, or I might be on the other side of the world when you move on. But if I'm alive and available, I'll take your funeral.' 'Good,' she said rather pre-emptively, 'I will put it in my will that your airfare will be paid.'

Though she had five years to go, it was only four months later that a peaceful death set her free and a joyful funeral celebrated her life.

Thirty Nine
The Garden of Eden

Hamish Montgomery was one of the most immediately trustworthy and gregarious of people. He was an artist and a counsellor employed by the Church of Scotland to oversee its counselling centre in Glasgow. His warmth, understanding and encouragement were a blessing to all whom he helped.

Once a year he was expected to give a report on the centre's work to the Presbytery of Glasgow, the regional government for Presbyterian churches in and around the city. This monthly meeting could be a predictably morose affair in which minutes of tedious committee meetings were recorded or debated, and erstwhile princes of the pulpit were sent with blessings into retirement.

Possibly to pep up the proceedings, when it came to the annual report of the work of the Tom Allan Centre, Hamish began not with an account of its work but with a story.

This is what he said:

'As we all know from the Bible, after God created Adam, he made Eve as a companion for him. Adam wasn't quite sure how to deal with this unprecedented arrival, so he asked God, 'What have I to do with Eve?'

'Love her,' God replied.

'What does that mean?' asked Adam.

'Just take her hand and go for a walk and see what transpires.'

So Adam and Eve walked about for an hour and then Adam said to God,

'Is love just about walking and holding hands?'

'No. There's more to it. Why don't you stop now and then and kiss Eve. That means putting your lips against hers.'

So off Adam went and, from time to time, he would stop to kiss Eve and then walk on. He turned to God again.

'God, my lips are sore with all this kissing. Is this all that love's about?'

'No, Adam. But I think you might be keeping back from Eve. Do the same again, but get a bit closer to each other and see what happens.'

At this point I could sense a ripple of apprehension running under the hard seats on which the reverend Presbyterian sages sat.

Soon after, Adam came back and asked, 'God, what's a headache?'

This conclusion was met with confusion. Some ministers pouted in righteous indignation, while others stuffed handkerchiefs in their mouths or dug their nails into their hands to suppress laughter at the best joke they had ever heard in religious precincts.

Forty
No easy answer

Compared to other similar establishments, it was late in the day that Glasgow University initiated a student counselling service. When I held the sabbatical office of President of the Students' Representative Council, one result was that occasionally students who had serious personal problems contacted me. This may have been aided and abetted by the fact that I was known to be studying theology.

One day a twenty-year-old male student asked to see me. He said that he wanted to tell me two things about which he had never spoken before to anyone. The first was that he felt called to the priesthood in a denomination very different from that in which he had been reared. The second was that he knew he was sexually attracted to young children.

I immediately felt inadequate for the conversation. I could deal with the first issue; but I had little knowledge of the second. However, I let him say what he needed to articulate.

He had grown up in a very narrow Calvinist family and, after adolescence, felt confirmed in his mind that he was gay. He spoke about this to his father, an academic who, in turn, referred his son privately to a psychiatrist who practised aversion therapy as a cure for homosexuality. This involved the boy, when in his mid-teens, having a device strapped to him which would give him an electric shock if he registered arousal on being shown pictures of naked men. No such shock was experienced when the photographs were of naked females. (Did the psychiatrist think this was a redemptive use of pornography?)

It hadn't worked. So now he was twenty. He had never engaged in sexual relations with another male, but he did know that he became aroused when he thought about engaging with children.

I asked if he had ever improperly touched a child, and he said,

'No.' Then I said to him, 'Why are you telling me this?' And he replied, 'Because I need to tell someone. It has been a horrible secret for too long. I want to declare to someone else that I will never harm a child as long as I live.'

After further conversation, I said to him, 'I want you to know that this conversation has been shared by you and me and God. This has been a holy space. And although I do not know your name and may never see you again, I will hold you accountable for what you have promised.'

In the next twenty years, I saw him twice in passing. He was ordained by that time and served as a curate and then a parish priest. He died as a result of an accident in his mid-forties, and his loss was mourned by the two communities which he had served, and in which he was held in great respect and affection. Since his death, and despite the publicity given to abusive behaviour by priests, no one in the parishes he served has ever made even a hint of accusation against him.

I wonder how many other potential offenders could be kept from crime, and how many hundreds of thousands of children would never be violated, if we rated prevention, including confidential counselling, as high a priority as the punishment of offenders.

Forty One
The song

In the late eighties, a group of ten young adults from Scotland went to the Kirchentag in Frankfurt, Germany. They joined another hundred or so people of similar age from all over the globe for a pre-event conference in a retreat house. Participants arrived on the eve of the conference, and were introduced to the proposed agenda.

On the first morning, everyone was encouraged to spend most of the time in groups of seven or eight, where the primary purpose was to share with each other something about themselves and the country from which they came.

In one group were two women from Southern Africa. Tarasai came from Zimbabwe. She spoke at length and with passion about the change in the country from being a former British colony to becoming an international pariah after Rhodesia (as it was formerly called) declared independence from Britain. It subsequently became an apartheid state in which the black majority population was ruled by the white minority.

A civil war had ensued in which Tarasai had been part of the people's liberation army which helped to destabilise the ruling establishment. This led ultimately to a democratic election which was won by the Zanu PF party, led by Robert Mugabe who consequently became president. Her talk gave a rare insight into the significance of women in the struggle against the white male hegemony.

Other people in the group spoke in turn and finally a woman from Namibia introduced herself and told of her nation. It was, at that time, a client state of South Africa. It was rich in minerals, but the profit from mining never made any difference to the local economy or the inhabitants. It was all funnelled into Pretoria. She expressed a helplessness which people felt at the exploitation of their nation, combined with South Africa's unwillingness to let them determine their own future.

As she spoke, there was a gentle sound of weeping. It came from Tarasai who listened very intently to all that the Namibian woman had to say.

When she had finished, Tarasai spoke. She said, 'While you have been speaking, I have been weeping. I feel for your pain; it is the pain which we too suffered in Zimbabwe. But I want to tell you that the God above you is more powerful than all the wickedness that surrounds you, and I am going to sing a song for you and your people.'

And then, with strength and utter conviction, Tarasai sang the song which had effectively been the Zimbabwean anthem of liberation, changing only one word to name the other nation.

> If you believe and I believe
> and we together pray,
> the Holy Spirit must come down
> and set Namibia free.
> and set Namibia free,
> and set Namibia free;
> the Holy Spirit must come down
> and set Namibia free.

Forty Two
The sunbeam

I did not know her name, but she struck me as one of the most beautiful women I had ever seen. And it wasn't because of her blonde hair and blue eyes, lovely though they were. It was the way in which she seemed to be at one with herself, comfortable in herself, easily and happily engaged in conversation with other people, smiling and self-effacing.

At the conference we attended, I hoped that at one mealtime I might be able to sit beside her. But it never happened; other people always got there first, until one lunchtime she sat down opposite me. She had a question she wanted to ask about a presentation I had given that morning. It concerned grieving.

We discussed her question amicably and then she said, 'Can I tell you a little about myself?' to which I gladly assented. She continued,

'My profession is – or was – nursing. I had always wanted to work in a hospital and care for people who were ill. So I did all the necessary training, and clearly made an impression as I was fairly quickly promoted to the post of theatre sister.

'One day, while assisting at an operation, the young surgeon and I locked eyes and began the kind of "medical romance" which features in movies. Like me, he was of Scandinavian stock with ancestors who came from Sweden to the USA and settled in the central states.

'We were quick off the mark in committing ourselves to each other. Barely three months of courting and we were engaged. Within a year we were married and within a week I was pregnant.

'We both looked forward to the birth of our first child. In those years there was no indication of the sex of the foetus. We would have been equally happy with a boy or a girl, and were sure that, like both of us, he or she would have blue eyes and blonde hair.

'I had a comparatively easy pregnancy, and when I went into labour it was not for long. But as soon as the baby was put in my arms, I realised that he would never be able to walk, never be able to move easily, and might never be able to say my name. I moaned, "This is not the baby I want."

'I rejected the child; I did not want to touch him; I went into a depression which continued until I found the strength to pray to God that I might learn to love the baby I had, and forget about the ideal baby I had wanted.

'That's almost thirty years ago and now not only is Jack my proud son, but also my closest friend. Although he cannot speak, he loves life. Every day has surprises for him, and he shares his delight with whoever is around.

'Just on Sunday past, I wheeled him into our church. As we moved down the aisle, a sunbeam struck one of the stained-glass windows and spattered Jack's white shirt with a kaleidoscope of colour. He whooped for joy and all the congregation applauded his delight.'

It seems an unusual thing to say, but I have often wondered in retrospect whether the wholesome beauty in that lovely woman had been deeply enhanced by the blessing of the child she almost rejected.

Forty Three
The linguist

In 1976 Charlotte Mackellar, a qualified physiotherapist in her mid-twenties, decided to leave Central Scotland and see the world.

She ended up in Amsterdam, a city about which she knew nothing, where shortage of cash persuaded her to seek suitable employment. Her only language was English, spoken with a distinctly West of Scotland accent. She applied to several hospitals and was interviewed. The only one which offered her a job was the last that she would have chosen. While she was glad of employment, she was less enthusiastic about the consequences.

It was made clear to her that, because she would be interacting daily with patients, the vast majority of whom were from the Netherlands, she would have to learn Dutch. To this she applied herself and was encouraged by meeting up with other young women from Scotland who were also employed in healthcare. Through them she became aware of the English Reformed Church in the middle of the city, which was a joint congregation of The Church of Scotland and The Netherlands Reformed Church.

At church, Charlotte met – among other people – a young man of around her own age who was called Lex van Schoor. He was extremely handsome, courteous and affectionate, and he worked in the aerospace industry. Before long they bonded, set up home and flew over to get married in Scotland with celebratory events for friends in both countries.

Soon after, they settled in Scotland where Lex found a compatible job. In a short time, their first child, Ingrid, was born. Her sister Morag followed not long after. Lex and Charlotte were keen that they should be bilingual. So while the girls spoke English outside, Lex spoke in Dutch with them at home. This went well until they started school. They couldn't really tell their dad what happened in class, because they didn't have the Dutch words. Thereafter, most conversation was in English.

Ten years later, their son Jules was born and soon there was another move, this time to Toulouse in France where Lex worked on the European Airbus project. He had a little French, but because the team he worked with were international in membership, English was often the common language.

Not so easy for Charlotte, who had to begin all over again to learn parts of the body and medical terminology in yet another language to enable her to have fulfilling therapist-to-patient conversations. But she persevered, and had the consolation of easier discourse in the English-speaking community church which they joined.

The family had a very happy home. The two girls each chose yet another language to study at university, German for Ingrid and Spanish for Morag. And Jules picked up bits and pieces of these languages while developing a very convincing French regional accent.

Time passed and one day Lex, having undergone medical investigation, was given a diagnosis of cancer, pervasive throughout his body. He was the model patient, never complaining or drawing attention to himself or his illness. Accepting that his time on Earth was clearly limited, he retired from work, pottered around the house, cooked meals and enjoyed the love and attention of Charlotte and their children.

After his death, given that all their offspring were pursuing work or education away from the family home, Charlotte moved back to Scotland with their approval. Ingrid began working in Germany and, when the time was right, let her mother know that she had become very friendly with Reza, a refugee from Iran. It became clear that their fondness was likely to move towards commitment.

Charlotte was happy to meet Ingrid's boyfriend, but all communication had to be done by translation as Reza spoke only Arabic and German. In the fullness of time, the couple became engaged and subsequently married.

It would be five years after they had first met that Charlotte flew to Cologne to see her daughter and son-in-law and greeted Reza with a distinctly German expression. He was quite taken aback that she spoke German so fluently. When he asked how this had happened, Charlotte's response brought tears to his eyes.

She simply said that she had – in her mid-sixties – studied for an Open University degree in French and German, so that she might easily communicate with her son-in-law and with any grandchildren she might yet have.

Forty Four
Jimmy

For a teenager, one of the joys in conversing with grandparents can be the discovery of society as it used to be: to be informed of what it was like to live during a world war; to learn of leaving school at fourteen or fifteen; to become aware that Britain before the NHS was a very different place; to hear of how your parents behaved when they were your age – all these things and more can be the fruits of interacting with generations born in decades long past.

This certainly was my experience in the conversations I had Monday to Friday for most of the years of my schooling, when I ate lunch with my father's parents. And it was my expectation when, in the church I attended, the teenagers were encouraged to visit older people in the congregation.

Hence a great disappointment when I first went to see Mrs Gilbert, a long-standing member of the congregation, a regular attender at morning worship, and an able-bodied seventy something. She lived in a gloomy house. A dull patterned wallpaper covered her living room, the curtains were half-closed, and a standard lamp with a low voltage bulb was positioned behind her chair which faced the television. Conversation was awkward. If I asked a question, the answer was often monosyllabic; if I ventured an opinion or alluded to something in the news, she nodded or grunted. There was never a curiosity expressed about my own life, though she might well have known my grandparents.

On my second visit, I was determined to engage in dialogue and had considered topics which might enable a lively conversation: shops which had disappeared from the main street; television programmes which she might enjoy; members of the church she had known for a long time. All these were met with minimal interest, evident in her response. Eventually, in desperation, I looked towards the television on top of which sat a photograph of a young man in a Royal Air Force uniform. 'I see you must know someone in the RAF,' I said.

This was like lighting a touch paper. Her eyes darkened, her face contorted, and through gritted teeth and pursed lips she spat out the words, 'That was Jimmy. The Germans got him over Dresden.'

I had heard enough from my father, who had been in the army at the end of the war and witnessed how the city of Dresden had been flattened by massive British bombing, to know that Jimmy had not been on a holiday flight. I learned subsequently that he had been a pilot whose aircraft was shot down, leading to his death and burial on foreign soil.

I had no idea how to respond. Her bereavement was not recent. It had happened over thirty years previously, but the bitterness in her voice could easily have suggested that it had occurred the previous week. Facing the television with Jimmy's photograph on top, there was no way in which, in her daily life, Mrs Gilbert could avoid remembering her lost son.

It was clear that her life had been put on hold. The fact that people involved in war die, and that there is no discrimination between the believers and the non-believers when a machine gun brings down an aircraft – such realities seemed never to have percolated into her consciousness. Not only were 'the Germans' damned in her estimation, but her other son, a local tradesman, was also affected. The dead boy had been the favourite son, and the living one was no replacement.

I often think of her. She is the Lot's wife of my teenage years, a person who gazes on destruction so keenly that she herself becomes immobilised.

Forty Five
Mexico

In 2005, the Church of Scotland published a new hymn book which had been almost ten years in the making. This was to replace a hymnal, then in current use, which had been produced in 1973, though it might as well have been published in 1873 for all the attention it paid to the twentieth century. The process took a long time partly because the Church's ruling body, the General Assembly, had wanted a committee of thirty people to work on it, whereas most other denominations would have had a panel of ten plus a secretary and external advisor.

The other reason that it took so long was simply because none of the members had ever been involved in producing a hymnal before. Indeed, the vast majority were only familiar with previous hymnals of their own denomination and had little interest in or experience of what was being sung in other parts of Christendom.

For the first three years, the members surveyed what had been sung in the past and subsequently deselected from the 1973 book almost two-thirds of the contents, on the grounds that these items were either rarely sung or now obsolete. They then began to look at materials from all over the world, not just from English-speaking nations, in an attempt to produce a volume which would reflect the theology, the interests and the cultures of both the local and global ecumenical community of which the Church of Scotland was a part. And they surveyed all such materials, innocent of the authorship of the items.

It transpired that the published volume included around eight percent of its content from outside the European/North American axis. Many of these were short songs, such as *Mungu Ni Mwema* (Know that God is good) from the Democratic Republic of the Congo. This was to create a smile as wide as an African sunrise on the face of a native of the Congo, present when the book was introduced to a congregation in Edinburgh.

Although it was anticipated that there might be a backlash from traditionalists whose sacred favourites had been expunged, there was virtually no dissent. The committee had indicated in advance which hymns from the 1973 book were being discontinued, and where correspondents offered substantial reasons for reversing any decision, items were readmitted.

Three years after publication, a letter was received from an elderly lady who lived on the east coast, not far from Edinburgh. This is what it said:

'I am writing to say that our church has been using the new hymn book for the last two years. In it there is a hymn which seemed to mean a lot to my husband; he would sometimes say, "That's a lovely song."

'I never thought much about it until three months ago when my husband died and my sons and I were making arrangements for his funeral. I said to the boys, "I must find that song which your dad liked; we should sing it." And before long I found it. So I just want to tell you how I thank God that someone I will never meet, whose language I have never spoken, and whose country I have never visited, wrote words which so perfectly enabled us to celebrate my husband's life here on earth and now in heaven.'

This is the song, originally written in Spanish and from Mexico:

* 1. When we are living, we are in the Lord,
    and when we're dying, we are in the Lord;
    for in our living and in our dying
    we belong to God, we belong to God.

2. Each day allows us to decide for good,
    loving and serving as we know we should;
    in thankful giving, in hopeful living,
    we belong to God, we belong to God.

3. Sometimes we sorrow, other times embrace,
   sometimes we question everything we face;
   yet in our yearning is deeper learning:
   we belong to God, we belong to God.

4. Till earth is over, may we always know
   love never fails us: God has made it so.
   Hard times will prove us, never remove us;
   we belong to God, we belong to God.

* *Original Spanish verse 1 Mexican traditional, verses 2-4 Roberto Escamilla (b. 1931) © Abingdon Press. English version copyright © 2002 WGRG, Iona Community, Glasgow, Scotland.*

Forty Six
Amnesty

Dawe Ackman was cruelly widowed while he was about the Lord's business.

He and his wife were members of an Anglican evangelical church in Cape Town, South Africa, which had a particular outreach to Russian sailors. No one was clear how this had begun, but it had become something of a tradition that when a Russian naval vessel docked in the local harbour, people from the congregation would organise to pick up the men who wanted to come to church, and drive them to the evening service.

On one particular Sunday, Dawe offered to drive the church minivan, while his wife and other members of the congregation picked up other sailors in their own cars. Through waiting for stragglers and heavy traffic on the roads, Dawe arrived later than his wife at the church. She was already inside the building, sitting beside those she had driven. It was a busy service with few empty seats, so Dawe had to sit at some distance from her.

Not long after the start of worship, there burst in through the main doors four black youths who threw hand grenades into the congregation and opened fire with pistols. They did not stay long, but fled leaving the congregation stunned and shocked that such a thing could have happened and that so many worshippers were wounded. Some people died, including Dawe's wife. He ran over to her, and held her in his arms as the life left her body.

Within minutes the crime scene was surrounded by police and army vehicles, and subsequently the media arrived to report on the dastardly incident. Dawe, still barely able to speak, was interviewed for television and asked if there was anything he would like to say. He stammered through a response, part of which indicated that, as he was a committed Christian, he had to forgive the murderers. The recording of that interview suggests that Dawe said these words not because he felt forgiveness well up within him, but because as a Christian he had to.

The four boys were eventually apprehended by the police and given long prison sentences for murder.

Years passed, and with the dawn of democracy came also the unprecedented decision to consider amnesties for people imprisoned during the years of conflict. The Truth and Reconciliation Commission, chaired by Archbishop Desmond Tutu, held hearings throughout the country at which those who were incarcerated could apply for amnesty.

The procedure was quite straightforward. At the hearings those who were the accused seeking amnesty were interrogated both by the panel of adjudicators and by the victims or relatives of the victims should they so wish. Such a hearing was organised in Cape Town where the four black assailants had asked for their case to be considered.

Along with other members of the congregation, Dawe went to the building where the hearing was being held, and saw opposite him the four boys, now young men, who had created mayhem in the church. After their request for amnesty had been rehearsed, Dawe was asked if he would like to ask any questions of the accused.

His first was, 'Do you know which of you killed my wife?' There was no positive reply. The four had not targeted specific people. They had just thrown hand grenades, shot their guns and fled.

He then asked, 'Do you know what it is like to lose your wife?' Again little could be said. None of the then boys had had a girlfriend, never mind a wife.

'Why did you do this?' was his third question, and one of the accused said, 'Because we were under orders, in the same way as the South African security forces were under orders. And if we or they were told to kill, then there were deaths.'

'Is there anything you want to say to me?' was his final question. It elicited this reply, 'Sir, we regret that we were the cause of your wife's death. But you have her grave. And you can go there to grieve for her and remember her. We have lost fathers and brothers and uncles, killed by the security forces, their bodies sometimes burned, sometimes thrown on rubbish heaps. There is no place for us to go and remember our losses.'

When he heard their truth, Dawe became completely convinced that he should agree to their being given freedom.

After the hearing, members of the congregation met with the four men, and prayed with them. Dawe spoke to and hugged each one of them. I asked him 'What did it feel like, knowing that you had embraced the man who killed your wife?' He replied, 'It was a great feeling of liberation.'

Forty Seven
The night visitor

Gaby de Wil lived on the ground floor of a multistorey block of flats in central Brussels. It was a mixed racial area with its fair share of poverty and criminality, sufficient for Gaby to take safety precautions. One of which was to leave a message in French and Arabic on her table on top of a small pile of bank notes. It read:

Please do not look for money in my house. There is none here. If you are in need, take the money I have left below this message. And may God bless you.

One evening, having had a fairly demanding day, Gaby went early to bed and fell fast asleep. She was wakened shortly after midnight by the buzzing of the intercom which linked her to the entrance foyer of the building. She asked who was calling her, and a voice replied, 'Jean-Paul.'

Jean-Paul was a man in his early fifties who was a vagrant. He had spent years in prison after being found guilty of murder, and though not a severe alcoholic, he sometimes became the worse for wear. His family had disowned him, but he had found a degree of acceptance in the Beguinage church where he occasionally turned up.

'Oh Jean-Paul,' said Gaby, 'I am very sorry, but I am in bed. I am so tired tonight. It would not be possible to have a conversation with you at this late hour. Perhaps I will see you later in the week.' Then she said goodbye and put the receiver down.

She put out the light and tried to get back to sleep. She began to turn over in her mind whether it had been right or wrong to send Jean-Paul away. She could find no peace until, in laying out her dilemma before her Maker, she said to God, 'If it is really important for Jean-Paul to speak to me, send him back and I will answer the door and let him in.'

Half an hour later, the intercom rang again and she let Jean-Paul, the convicted murderer, come into the small two-roomed flat where she lived alone.

He sat down and began to spill out his woes: how he felt helpless as well as homeless; how his family wanted nothing to do with him; how he had no job or any hope of a job; nor did he have many people whom he could count as friends.

Gaby listened patiently for well nigh forty minutes, letting him rehearse his troubles. When he had finished, she was at odds as to how to reply. 'Oh Jean-Paul,' she said, 'I don't know how I can help you. I am an old woman. I do not have much money or any influence. Only Jesus Christ is able to help you.'

At that, Jean-Paul looked at her, picked up his hat to make clear that he was ready to leave, and then he said with abject conviction, 'Tonight, Gaby, you have been Jesus Christ for me.'

Forty Eight
Light in the tunnel

For most of her married life, Alison's identity was closely associated with her husband's vocation. He was a minister and she a minister's wife. He was a kenspeckle, articulate and independently-minded individual who, during his ministry, made a significant impact on the parishes and the denomination he served.

She, a graduate in geography and a qualified school teacher, was also a musician with considerable instrumental skills on the piano and violin. But with the advent of her three children and expectations regarding the hospitality of the manse, her avocational interests took a back seat.

... Until in her fifties, after their three children had left the nest, she decided to study for the degree of Bachelor of Music. The oldest student among a batch of teenagers, she was welcomed into their fold, acquiring 'street-cred' by sight-reading the piano accompaniment to a lengthy cantata as the class sang. To her skill and enthusiasm for music, she added further capacities for composing and text writing.

Once graduated, and with a 2/1 honours degree, Alison began work on a church-related project regarding stained glass. She took to this like a duck to water. This led ultimately to her setting up a Symposium on stained glass at work, which in turn led to the creation of an independent Scottish Charity, The Scottish Stained Glass Trust.

After she and her husband retired from manse life into a home of their own, Alison developed a series of fast-growing cancers, first in her ankle and eight months later in her groin. Both were successfully removed by substantial operations.

One evening, I returned home late to find a message left the day before on my answering machine. It was quite brief: 'John, this is Charlie. It's quite urgent and it's about Alison.' Because it was nearing midnight, I deferred phoning her husband until the following morning. 'I'm quite glad you didn't phone,' he said, 'for we might have been discussing a funeral.' He then briefly informed me that Alison was in hospital again having had a large operation, and I decided to go that afternoon to see her.

Alison looked like a wee sparrow in her bed, frail and attached to a battery of tubes and drips, but smiling when she recognised me. 'What are you doing in here?' I asked. Then she told her story.

'I suddenly became very unwell. I knew it was something internal. I went with Charlie to the doctor, who, knowing my medical history, had me admitted to hospital right away. After a week of tests, the consultant came to me with the news that I had a sizeable tumour all over my small intestine. He said that he could not provide me with any betterment by means of surgery or anything else. I lay there that day and thought hard about what it meant to be "inoperable". Later that evening, when the senior consultant came round with a bunch of medical students in tow, he asked me how I was. I said, "I understand what you are telling me and that I will die of this tumour. I am not asking for the impossible. But I *am* asking you to try to give me some time, because I have not seen my children; and also because I need to call a meeting of the Scottish Stained Glass Trust. They can come here, but I have to impress upon them that they have to raise a lot of money to employ somebody to do my work, otherwise all our research of the last six years will be wasted."

'He said it was so complicated inside my body that he did not know what to advise; but as he left it was clear to me that he would be talking it over with his students and the young surgeon.

'Next morning, early, my prospective surgeon came and offered me a bypass operation that might give me a little extra time but would not save my life, and I decided to accept it. That evening after I came round, the surgeon told me he had just rung my husband to say, "I've left the boys sewing her up. We got it all out." And so there I was, pieced together, with "a very large hole in the middle".

Within months, Alison was back collating information on stained-glass installations, enthusing people up and down the country, and playing and writing words and music.

Here is one of her early hymns, which has featured on *Songs of Praise*, and been of great significance to people experiencing hard times or facing change in their future.

> Love is the touch of intangible joy;
> love is the force that no fear can destroy;
> love is the goodness we gladly applaud:
> God is where love is, for love is of God.
>
> Love is the lilt in a lingering voice;
> love is the hope that can make us rejoice;
> love is the cure for the frightened and flawed:
> God is where love is, for love is of God.
>
> Love is the light in the tunnel of pain;
> love is the will to be whole once again;
> love is the trust of a friend on the road:
> God is where love is, for love is of God.
>
> Love is the Maker and Spirit and Son;
> love is the kingdom their will has begun;
> love is the pathway the saints all have trod:
> God is where love is, for love is of God.

Words copyright © 1998 Alison Robertson

Forty Nine
The bill

Someone, whose name was not appended, sent me this account of an incident in which she had been involved. I do no more than represent her words.

'I took Colin out for a meal in a nearby restaurant. As we had not booked, they were very sorry that there was no table available. However, the young vivacious waitress was overruled by her boss who organised a small table in the middle of the restaurant. Good food, good service, good company, animated conversation, laughter all around. I had not seen Colin for a while.

'As the meal ended, I requested the bill from the waitress. She bent down and said with a giggle, "It's been taken care of." My eyes widened as I looked at Colin. He shook his head.

'"WHAT?" I exclaimed. The waitress pointed to a man on a window seat, who was smiling and looking at me, and she repeated, "It has been taken care of."

'I smiled back; he came over and said he thought he should explain. His wife, sitting next to him, had been watching us. She was dying of cancer, and was so taken with our demeanour and laughter that she asked her husband to pay for our meal. It was two days before Mother's Day and she was sure we were mother and son.

'I was flabbergasted, so I muttered, "Thank you." By this time she was looking at me. I got up, as did she, and gave her a hug which she returned. No words would come; she began to cry and so did I. We were taken aback and deeply moved. I keep remembering it, and wonder how this unknown couple are.'

Fifty
Transference

When Howard Anderson told his parents that he felt called to be a minister, his father, a university senior lecturer, said, 'What a waste of a magnificent brain.' His mother simply smiled. He remembered that poignant moment all his life, and particularly after his father died.

It was an unexpected announcement, since Howard had never shown much interest in religion. Indeed his father positively discouraged it. But otherwise, he was a good father, encouraging his son's academic and sporting prowess, ensuring the family had interesting holidays together, and showing generosity when it came to pocket money.

It was at university that Howard came into touch with Christianity through taking religious studies as a subsidiary subject in his arts degree. He became not only interested but committed, after involvement in a friendly church. He was baptised and confirmed and – after discerning a vocational call – he offered himself for ordination and was accepted by the Church of Scotland.

He sailed through his divinity course, ministered in two churches in mainland Scotland, then crossed the Atlantic to serve two churches in the Presbyterian tradition in the USA. He kept in contact with his parents and visited them whenever he could.

On hearing that his father was poorly and coming near his end, Howard decided to fly back to Glasgow to be with his parents. His father was very appreciative; he and Howard spoke frankly about many things. This afforded Howard the opportunity to ask his dad about his lifelong disapproval of religion.

His father told how he had been orphaned as a young boy and sent to live in a children's home run by a Christian charity. In his adolescent years he became the object of unwelcome sexual advances by male members of staff. Eventually he decided to make a break for it, ran away from the children's home and – at an early age – vowed that if he ever became a parent, he would ensure that his children had nothing to do with any organisation which smacked of religion.

This was important for Howard to hear. It answered questions he had long pondered, and it ensured that when his father died, there was no unfinished business between them, and certainly no animosity.

Howard stayed for several days after his dad's funeral to help his mother with the legal and business things that are the unwelcome but necessary concomitants of a death. In the course of their conversations, he asked his mother why, when years ago he had indicated that he felt called to the ministry, she – unlike his father – had smiled at the news.

She told him something which had been hidden in her heart since the day he was born.

When she first met Howard's father, he was a soldier in uniform, recently demobbed from the army after being in National Service. They sat next to each other on a bus as she was returning home from her work. He asked if they might meet again later, and she told him that she was going to a meeting in the city for the early part of the evening. He arranged to meet her after her engagement.

The meeting she attended was an interview for women interested in becoming deaconesses – one of the few possibilities the church at that time held for women who felt called to full-time service. Ordination was still twenty years away. She told the young soldier of her vocational hopes, and he made no response. But during their courtship, when it became clear that they were moving towards a permanent commitment, George made it clear that if they married, he would not countenance any children born to them being associated with a church. His wife-to-be meekly assented.

Within a year of marriage, the pair were looking forward to the birth of their first child. After his birth, as was the practice of the time, babies spent only a part of the day in the presence of their mother. They were put for a few hours in a separate nursery to give the mothers some rest.

It happened that an Episcopalian priest walked through the ward in which Howard's mother had a bed. He noticed her weeping and, fearing that she had perhaps had a miscarriage or that there had been a perinatal death, he spoke with her. She revealed to him her distress at having to forfeit the calling she once felt keenly. And she spoke of her sadness at not being able to talk to her son about Jesus, or encourage him to grow up in the church, because of the agreement she had made with her husband.

The priest then asked if he could see the baby. Accordingly Howard was brought to him. He held him and opened a small bottle containing oil for anointing. Having dipped his finger in it, he made the sign of the cross on Howard's tiny forehead and said to his mother, 'God will never forfeit a vocation.'

Wild Goose Publications, the publishing house of the Iona Community established in the Celtic Christian tradition of Saint Columba, produces books, e-books, CDs and digital downloads on:

- holistic spirituality
- social justice
- political, peace and environmental issues
- healing and wellbeing
- innovative approaches to worship
- song in worship, including the work of the Wild Goose Resource Group
- material for meditation and reflection

Visit our website at
www.ionabooks.com
for details of all our products and online sales